Tracing Ancestors

in

BARBADOS

A Practical Guide

By Geraldine Lane

GENEALOGICAL PUBLISHING CO., INC.

Second printing, 2007

Published by Genealogical Publishing Company
3600 Clipper Mill Rd., Suite 260
Baltimore, MD 21211-1953
Library of Congress Catalogue Card Number 2005935116
ISBN-10: 0-8063-1765-5
ISBN-13: 978-0-8063-1765-6
Made in the United States of America

To
Matthew and Joanne

Contents

List of Illustrations

Preface

When, as an experienced genealogist, I arrived in Barbados in 1999, I was pleased at the prospect of spending a few years researching Barbadian families. I soon discovered that despite the effects of a tropical climate, hurricanes and fires, a good supply of records survives on the island. Continuous ownership of Barbados by England from settlement in 1627 to independence in 1966 gives continuity to the records, and they are similar to those created in England. My training with the Institute of Heraldic & Genealogical Studies in Canterbury, England, had prepared me well for the task ahead. The most recent guide to records in Barbados, I discovered, was C.J. Stanford's *Genealogical Sources in Barbados*, published in *The Genealogists' Magazine* in England in March 1974. Though comprehensive, this guide was in need of updating, so I set about compiling a guide for my own use. Interest in Barbadian family history has grown enormously over recent years, and I feel it is now time to share my guide with others.

My aim in compiling this book is to help those with Barbadian origins to trace their ancestry. It is designed to guide the reader through the many types of records and published sources that record the lives of the people of Barbados. The novice will find this work to be a comprehensive guide, and the more experienced researcher may discover sources of which they were previously unaware. Those seeking the help of a local researcher will have an idea of what is available and be better able to direct his or her work.

When undertaking family history research, some ancestors are easier to trace than others. In Barbados the planter families with their wealth, land and influence feature more frequently in records. Some indentured servants stayed for a few years and then moved on to try their luck elsewhere; these may have passed through without a mention. Before they gained their freedom, slaves were rarely recorded, although the task for the researcher becomes easier after emancipation. This book aims to cover records relating to all sections of Barbadian society, to describe them in detail and highlight possible problems.

The focus is on records held locally in Barbados, with an account of Internet and published sources relating to them and to records held elsewhere. Guy Grannum, in his excellent book *Tracing Your West Indian Ancestors*, describes sources for Barbados held in England. Thus these records have not been included here; the two books will be complementary.

The world of genealogy is constantly changing. Records available on the Internet in particular increase at a great rate, and others become available in print. Some old records become too fragile to be seen and have to be withdrawn from public access. Others are repaired when time and money allow and so become more accessible. This book is a snapshot of records available at the time of writing, and I would be happy to hear from anyone with news of any changes.

Geraldine Lane
Barbados 2005
GeraldineTLane@hotmail.com

Acknowledgments

Compiling a book of this type requires the assistance of many people; to all those listed here, I would like to express my very sincere thanks.

For their time, patience and advice: Betty Carillo Shannon and Paulette Gooding at the Library of the Barbados Museum & Historical Society; Christine Matthews, David Williams and Ingrid Marshall at the Barbados Department of Archives; Sylvia Reynolds at the National Library Service; Avril Sealy at the Registration Department; and Carlyle Best at the Library of the University of the West Indies, Cave Hill.

For their encouragement and interest in the project: Dr Trevor Carmichael, Alissandra Cummins, Kathleen Drayton and Murcot Wiltshire.

For their kindness and generosity in answering my many questions on their various specialist subject areas: Warren Alleyne, Major-General John Graham, Guy Grannum, Ronnie Hughes, Michael McConway, Commander Michael Seakins, Dr Karl Watson and Dr Pedro Welch.

For their encouragement and practical help in various ways: Richard Goddard, Marlene Husbands, Pat Stafford, Jenny Swainston, Brenda Tate-Lovery and Jean Walker.

For their helpful suggestions: my fellow researchers Carol King and Lila Salazar.

For her expert editing skills: Alison Gaunt.

My friends Maris Corbin and Mary Gleadall deserve a special mention for welcoming me to the Barbados family history scene when I arrived on the island some years ago. Our shared interests have given us much pleasure, and their support and practical help with this project have been invaluable.

Finally, I would like to thank my husband, Robert, whose loyal support, good humor and unflagging patience have helped me to get this book written.

Introduction

Barbados, the most easterly of the Caribbean islands, measures 21 miles by 14 miles, with a land area of 166 square miles and a present-day population of more than 250,000.

The first English ship to arrive in 1625 found an uninhabited island, which had been abandoned by its Amerindian settlers 100 years previously. Two years later the ship *William & John* arrived, bringing the first English settlers; from that date until independence in 1966 the island remained an English possession.

By the 1650s a flourishing sugar industry meant that the island was the wealthiest colony in the British Empire. Fortunes were to be made and a variety of immigrants arrived, from sons of the wealthy to indentured servants. Convicts and political rebels were dispatched to the island, and the growing need for labor on the plantations gave rise to a profitable Atlantic trade in African slaves.

Many of the early white settlers and their descendants, among them disenchanted farmers and former servants, moved on to pursue new opportunities in other Caribbean islands and the Americas. This migration continued over the centuries as new opportunities arose. Following full emancipation in 1838, those formerly held in slavery joined the ranks of the emigrants; in the following years thousands headed for Trinidad, British Guiana, Suriname, and the Panama Canal project. Others went to Cuba, Costa Rica, Curaçao, Honduras and Nicaragua; by the 1920s the USA was the most popular destination.

In recent years the popularity of family history research has increased dramatically, particularly in countries with a history of immigration from Barbados. Descendants of these early settlers are now keen to discover their origins, and in many cases their search will lead them to the records in Barbados.

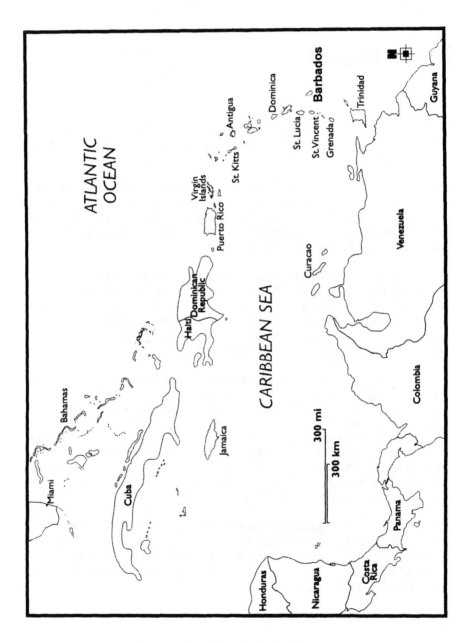

Figure 1   Map of the Caribbean

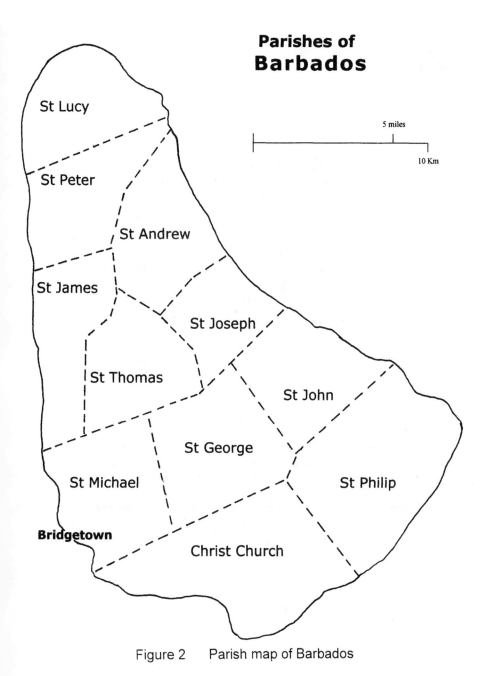

Parishes of
Barbados

St Lucy

St Peter

St Andrew

St James

St Joseph

St Thomas

St John

St George

St Michael

St Philip

Bridgetown

Christ Church

5 miles

10 Km

Figure 2   Parish map of Barbados

Glossary

Bajan	Barbadian.
Creole	A person born in the West Indies. In Barbados, the term is used for people of both European and African descent.
Emancipation	Freedom from slavery.
Indentured servant	A person legally bound to serve a master or mistress for a certain number of years. An exchange of food, clothing and shelter was provided, with the promise of a piece of land at the end of their contract. In reality, few were granted land.
Manumission	The granting of freedom from slavery.
Mulatto	A person of mixed black and white parentage.
Negro	An African or a person of African descent.
Redlegs	White indentured servants who fell on hard times (the name deriving from their sunburned legs), otherwise known as "poor whites."
West Indies	Used synonymously with Caribbean and sometimes extended to include Bermuda, the Bahamas islands, British Honduras (now Belize) and British Guiana (now Guyana).

Chapter 1

Getting started

An advantage of genealogy as a hobby is that you can pick it up and put it down depending on how much spare time you have. Your ancestors are not going anywhere and will still be there waiting for you when you have a couple of weeks to spend on them or the free time we all hope for in retirement.

The first steps described here can be taken at any time without the need to set foot in any archives. The information gathered can be tucked away and will provide a good starting point for further research.

First steps

Begin with yourself and work backwards one generation at a time, i.e. always work from the known to the unknown.

Talk to your relatives and any close friends of the family and try to gather as much of the following information as possible about your parents and grandparents:
- Full names and nicknames or pet names
- Dates and places of birth and marriage
- Dates and places of death and burial and whether there is a gravestone
- Religions and occupations
- Service in World Wars I and II and any other military service, including names of regiments
- Dates and places where people lived
- Brothers and sisters and their order in the family
- Family stories and gossip (take them with a pinch of salt until you have further proof!)
- Family connections in other countries and whether family members have emigrated

The next step is to gather all old letters and diaries; documents such as birth and marriage certificates; wills; family Bibles, which may have details of family births, marriages and deaths in them; press cuttings and heirlooms to see what they can tell you about your family history. Identify people in photographs and establish how they fit into the family.

Record everything you learn and where the information came from. As your records grow you may wish to invest in one of the many computer programs designed for recording this type of information. See what's available at **www.genealogysupplies.com**. Alternatively, a good card index system can work well.

Ancestors are not just a list of names and dates, and as research progresses you will learn more about the lives they led. Some knowledge of the history of Barbados is helpful at this stage, and you will find some recommended reading at the end of this chapter. For those on the island a visit to the Barbados Museum is an enjoyable and informative experience.

Some points to keep in mind

If you're interested in more than one of your lines of descent, choose the most uncommon name to start your research.

The spelling of surnames varies enormously so be flexible in your approach. Officials recorded names as they heard them, and as the majority of the population could not read or write, they could not correct the spelling.

Be aware of different first names. Some people are known by nicknames, pet names or use their second name in preference to the first name under which they were officially recorded at birth.

As in many other countries children have been, and still are, born out of wedlock in Barbados. This can cause difficulty in tracing their records. At birth they will have been registered with the mother's surname, and the father will not have been recorded. In some cases these children later took their father's name or another surname, and this name may appear on their marriage or burial certificates.

It can be very difficult to trace descendants of slaves in the period before emancipation in 1834. Slaves were the personal property of their owners and do not often appear in records. There are some sources for this period, however, and these are described in the "Slave records" chapter.

BDA: Barbados Department of Archives; BML: Barbados Museum Library

Local records are often incomplete, having suffered damage from climate, insects and neglect.

Websites and indexes can have mistakes in them. Always check any data taken from them against the original records wherever possible.

The staffs in libraries and archives are not there to do your research for you: their role is to provide you with and give guidance on the records and publications you wish to consult. Always prepare well for a visit and arrive with a list of the items you hope to see.

As the family historian you will soon accumulate a collection of important documents, and family members may entrust you with the care of photographs, Bibles and other heirlooms. With a little attention to their preservation, you can ensure that they survive for future generations to enjoy.

Next steps

Having done your initial research you are now ready to look further. See Appendix 1 for a timeline of the principal records available for researchers. Records in Barbados of interest to family historians are held in five places. These are described in detail in the "List of archives" chapter and are as follows:

Barbados Department of Archives (BDA)
Shilstone Memorial Library at the Barbados Museum (BML)
National Library Service (NLS)
Library of the University of the West Indies, Cave Hill Campus
Registration Department

The abbreviated form used in this book for the first three will become familiar to the reader. Most published sources mentioned can be found on their shelves, and this is indicated in brackets in each case.

Further reading

Beckles, Hilary. *A History of Barbados: from Amerindian settlement to nation-state* (BDA, BML, NLS)

Campbell, P.F. *An Outline of Barbados History* (BDA, BML)

Hoyos, F.A. *Barbados: A History from the Amerindians to Independence* (BDA, BML, NLS)

Chapter 2

Important dates in the history of Barbados

Date	Event
1536	Portuguese explorer Pedro a Campo landed on Barbados and was the first European to record a visit to the island. He named the island but did not settle.
1625 May 14	British Sea Captain John Powell visited Barbados and claimed the island on behalf of King James I.
1627	Captain Henry Powell, John's brother, brought the first English settlers to Barbados on the ship *William & John*.
1628	Followers of the Earl of Carlisle arrived on the island and claimed ownership for the Earl.
1629	Two years after the arrival of the settlers, 1,600 people were living on Barbados.
1640s	Sugar production replaced tobacco, cotton and indigo. The large-scale importation of African slaves began.
1675 Aug 31	Hurricane.
1680	The population had grown to approximately 20,000 whites and 38,000 black slaves.

NLS: National Library Service; JBMHS: Journal of the Barbados Museum & Historical Society

Date	Event
1731 Aug 13	Hurricane.
1780 Oct 10	Hurricane.
1807 Mar 25	Slave trade abolished.
1816 Apr 14	Bussa's Slave Rebellion.
1831 Aug 10/11	The Great Hurricane.
1833 Aug 28	Emancipation Act passed.
1834 Aug 1	Emancipation Act became effective but slaves were granted only conditional freedom. An apprenticeship system was established, requiring slaves to continue to work for their master.
1838 Aug 1	The apprenticeship scheme was abolished, and emancipation became a reality.
1845 Feb 3	Serious fire in Bridgetown.
1854	Cholera epidemic killed more than 20,000 people.
1860 Feb 14	Second serious fire in Bridgetown.
1898 Sep 10	Hurricane.
1955 Sep 22	Hurricane.
1959	The vestry system was abolished, ending the parish as unit of local government.
1966 Nov 30	Barbados became an independent state.

Chapter 3

List of archives

The Barbados Department of Archives (BDA)

Address	Black Rock St James Barbados
Telephone	(246) 425 1380 & 425 1381
Email	archives@sunbeach.net
Website	No
Opening hours	Mon–Fri, 8.30 a.m.– 4.15 p.m.
Entry charge	No
Facilities for the disabled	Good access to search room but a few steps to restroom facilities
Parking	In front of the building (free)
Restrooms	Yes
Food facilities	Covered area outside with tables and chairs; no food & drink for sale
Bag arrangements	Bags are left on shelves in the search room
Microfiche readers	Two; no advance booking arrangements
Microfilm readers	Three; no advance booking arrangements
Copying facilities	No
Digital camera use	Permitted for some records, at the discretion of the staff
Laptop computer plug-in facility	Yes
Internet connection for use of researchers	Yes but staff have priority
On-line catalog	No
Paid research availability	Staff do not carry out research but will provide a list of researchers
Other comments	No pens are allowed in the search room; pencils only

The Library of the Barbados Museum & Historical Society (BML)

Address	St Ann's Garrison St Michael Barbados
Telephone	(246) 427 0201
Email	museum@caribsurf.com
Website	www.barbmuse.org.bb/
Opening hours	Mon–Fri, 9 a.m.–1 p.m.
Entry charge	BMHS members free Non-member Barbados residents B$11.50 Non-member visitors B$23
Facilities for the disabled	None; the Library is upstairs
Parking	In front of the Museum (free)
Restrooms	Yes
Food facilities	Picnics can be taken outside in courtyard; no food & drink for sale
Bag arrangements	Bags are checked in at the library entrance
Microfiche readers	Not applicable
Microfilm readers	Not applicable
Copying facilities	Photocopier, B$0.86 per copy
Digital camera use	Not permitted
Laptop computer plug-in facility	Yes
Internet connection for use of researchers	No
On-line catalog	No
Paid research availability	Small research requests are carried out at a cost of US$10 per hour (minimum charge US$20) plus copying cost and postage
Other comments	The Library is kept at a cold temperature and a jacket or cardigan is advisable

The National Library Service (NLS)

Address	Coleridge Street Bridgetown Barbados
Telephone	(246) 426 1486
Email	natlib1@caribsurf.com reference@caribsurf.com
Website	No
Opening hours	Mon–Sat, 9 a.m.–5 p.m.
Entry charge	No
Facilities for the disabled	No
Parking	In library car park on right of building (free) or public car park opposite (B$1 per hour)
Restrooms	Yes
Food facilities	Picnic tables outside in courtyard area (no protection from sun or rain); no food & drink for sale
Bag arrangements	Bags are checked in and left at the entrance in a supervised area
Microfiche readers	Not applicable
Microfilm readers	There are two and advance booking is possible and advisable
Copying facilities	Microfilm copier and photocopier, both B$0.35 per copy (check in advance whether this facility is available)
Digital camera use	Not permitted
Laptop computer plug-in facility	No
Internet connection for use of researchers	No
On-line catalog	No
Paid research availability	Small research requests are carried out (for overseas enquirers only) at a cost of US$10 plus copying cost and postage
Other comments	Sources in this guide that can be found at the NLS are located in the reference section, above the lending library

The Library of the University of the West Indies

Address	Cave Hill St Michael Barbados
Telephone	(246) 417 4440
Email	mlrefdesk@uwichill.edu.bb
Website	http://mainlibrary.uwichill.edu.bb
Opening hours	Mon–Fri, 9 a.m.–5 p.m.
Entry charge/arrangements	Non-members of the University should seek permission and a charge is payable
Facilities for the disabled	Yes
Parking	Yes (free)
Restrooms	Yes
Food facilities	Yes
Bag arrangements	Bags are checked in at the Library entrance
Microfilm readers	One; booking advisable
Microfiche readers	One; booking advisable
Copying facilities	Yes
Laptop computer plug-in facility	Yes
Paid research availability	No

The Barbados Registration Department

Address	Supreme Court of Barbados Law Courts Coleridge Street Bridgetown Barbados
Telephone	(246) 426 3461
Fax	(246) 426 2405
Email	No
Website	No
Opening hours	Mon–Fri, 8.30 a.m.– 4 p.m.
Facilities for the disabled	No
Parking	Public car park opposite (B$1 per hour)

Chapter 4

Has it been done before?

Before starting your research it's worth asking yourself the question "Has it been done before?" Some Barbadian families have been researched thoroughly in the past and the results published or deposited so that others can have access to them. Your family names may be among these, or there could be someone currently researching your names who would be delighted to hear from you and happy to share information.

The Internet

Message Boards
Try a search of these message boards. They all relate specifically to Barbadian genealogy and messages posted from the start (as early as 1998) can be seen. They have search facilities so you can check for messages that include your surnames.

Barbados Genealogy Forum
http://genforum.genealogy.com/barbados/

Ancestry message boards
http://boards.ancestry.com/
Select "Barbados" in the "Find a message board" link.

Barbados Message Board
http://axses.com/encyc/bta/messages/
Select "Genealogy" from the list of options.

Surnames Index
The Caribbean Surnames Index can be seen at:
http://www.candoo.com/surnames/index.html
This site is managed by Jim Lynch, an important contributor to Barbadian genealogy through his website and publications. The site

---

aims simply to put those interested in a surname in touch with others. A quick search of the alphabetical list will tell you if there is someone out there you may wish to contact and whether their email address is supplied. It's worth checking this site frequently as names are added all the time, or you could add your own names and contact details.

Mailing List
http://archiver.rootsweb.com/th/index/caribbean
Similar to the message boards, this is a place where researchers post details of their interests and share information. The above address will show you the messages posted on the Caribbean List since about 1996. The list covers the whole Caribbean. For more information about how to join, visit the following site:
www.rootsweb.com/~caribgw/mailinglist.html

Website of The Church of Jesus Christ of Latter-day Saints (The Mormons)
http://www.familysearch.org
The LDS Church has filmed important genealogical records and collected a great deal of genealogical information from various sources. This is all brought together on their website and made available to researchers free of charge. A search for a surname specifying "Barbados" will reveal any research for your name submitted to the LDS Family History Department and placed in their Ancestral File. By selecting "all resources" when making a search, mentions of the name in the US census of 1880 and the Canadian and British censuses of 1881 will be revealed, among other sources. Probably the most important of these is the Barbados parochial registers of baptism and marriage, which were filmed and included in the International Genealogical Index (IGI). We look at this in more detail in Chapter 6.

Family information held at the Barbados Museum Library

The Family Files

The Museum Library has a large collection of material relating to Barbadian families. Organized alphabetically by surname, the contents of the files vary enormously. There is correspondence between researchers and those employing them. Private research has been donated, sometimes including a family tree covering centuries with detailed notes of those included in the tree. The Holder family is a good example of this. For others there are just a few sheets of notes or the odd letter. But even these can sometimes prove useful.

The Shilstone Collection

Eustace Maxwell Shilstone (1889–1969) was a Founder of the Barbados Museum & Historical Society and its library is named after him. Mr Shilstone was a great collector of information on Barbados families and the island's history. His collection of notebooks is held at the Museum Library and is a valuable resource for family historians. The information is mainly taken from the records at the BDA, and you can save a great deal of time by checking here first. There is a wealth of other information that would not easily be found elsewhere, for instance copies of entries in the Elcock family Bible 1755–1846. Many of the notebooks are written in pencil and the handwriting is not the easiest to decipher, but the effort will usually pay off. The Library has an index to the main family notebooks.

The Campbell Note Books

Mrs Diana Campbell's genealogical notes are contained in a collection of ring binders. They mainly consist of records of baptism, marriage and burial as well as wills and deeds compiled from records at the BDA. Organized alphabetically by surname, for some there are just a few notes and for others many pages. This is a well-organized, easily accessible collection.

Family information held at the Barbados Department of Archives

The BDA holds a collection of correspondence between family history researchers and enquirers. The collections were compiled by Ms Jill Hamilton, Ms Joy Hunt, Mr Harold G. Hutchinson and Ms Hilda Ince. These are kept in box files and are freely available on the shelves in the reading room. They are organized alphabetically by family, and the usefulness of the contents varies, ranging from a small amount of correspondence to a file full of data. The BDA "Names" card index file will direct you to these and other sources in the Archives collection.

Published sources

Family histories

Some family historians publish their work and distribute copies to family members; fortunately some are also generously donated to archives and libraries.

An excellent example of this is *The Hutchinson and Edghill Families of Barbados (1595–1995)* compiled by Herb Hutchinson and his father, Karl, covering fourteen generations of the family. Copies can be seen at the BDA and BML.

Other published family histories at the BML are Cheesman, Gittens, Hassell, Hutchins, Leacock, Lewis, Marshall, McConney, Moseley/Mosley, Pollard, Webster. The NLS has Trotman and Walcott.

There is no available listing for the BDA but a search in their "Names" card index will reveal whether they hold a history for a particular name.

Brandow, James C. (compiler). *Genealogies of Barbados Families* **(BDA, BML)**
This book brings together a collection of family histories published over time in Vere Langford Oliver's *Caribbeana* and the *Journal of the Barbados Museum & Historical Society*. It covers more than seventy families, and a comprehensive index makes this book useful for many other family names in addition to those of the main families studied. Every name mentioned is included even if the person's sole role in the family was simply to witness a will.

The *Journal of the Barbados Museum & Historical Society* (JBMHS)
Since it began publication in 1933 the *Journal* has published histories of Barbados families. As mentioned above, some of these are repeated in James Brandow's book. Those not included (from 1982 onwards) can be seen in the *Journal* and are as follows:

Walrond (Vols. 38, 39, 46), Clarke (Vol. 40), Rudder (Vol. 43), Oxnard (Vol. 47), Hogshard (Vol. 48), Lascelles (Vol. 50).

The *JBMHS* and *Caribbeana* are looked at in detail in the next chapter.

Chapter 5

The Journal of the Barbados Museum & Historical Society and Caribbeana

These two publications are of such value to family historians that they deserve a special mention.

The Journal of the Barbados Museum & Historical Society (JBMHS)

The Barbados Museum & Historical Society was formed in 1933 and in November of the same year the first issue of the Society's *Journal* was published. Articles relating to the cultural, historical and environmental heritage of Barbados have been published in more than 50 journals since that date.

The great value of the *Journal* for the family historian is that a personal name index has been compiled over the years. A search in this index for a particular name will give a list of all the volumes containing that name, plus the relevant page numbers. The researcher may find a complete family history, extracts from newspaper notices of baptism, marriage or death, obituaries, coroners' inquests, business advertisements and numerous other possibilities. A search in the index can save a great deal of time and is well worth doing in the early stages of your research.

The BML holds a full set of the *Journals* along with an up-to-date personal name index. The BDA and NLS also hold full sets though their personal name indexes cover early issues only.

NLS: National Library Service; JBMHS: Journal of the Barbados Museum & Historical Society

In addition to the personal name index, there is also a subject index to the *Journal*. This is another great time saver, as it lists every subject covered, whether in detail in a full article or just briefly in a passing reference. Some examples of entries are: Fairchild Street, Fairy Valley, Fires, Foundling Hospital, Freemasonry and Friends, Society of. After gathering some details of an ancestor's life, this would be a good place to look for further information.

The BML currently holds a subject index covering Vols. 1–48. The BDA and NLS hold printed subject indexes for Vols. 1–36, copies of which can be purchased from the Museum.

The current *Journal* is on sale in bookshops in Barbados and the Museum shop. Back copies, with a few exceptions, are still available and can be purchased in the Museum shop or ordered direct from the Museum. Contact details can be found in the "List of archives" chapter.

Caribbeana

Vere Langford Oliver was a great collector of Caribbean genealogical information and his findings were published between 1910 and 1919 in six volumes. The contents include transcriptions of parish registers, wills and deeds, pedigrees and extracts from newspapers. Some monumental inscriptions in England relating to West Indians are included as well as some unusual records such as matriculated students of the University of Glasgow from the West Indies. The volumes cover the entire Caribbean and there is a full name index.
This important work was reprinted by Jim Lynch in 2000. See **http:// www.candoo.com/olivers/caribbeana.html**.

The reprinted volumes can be seen at the BML. Copies of the original publication are available for reference at the BDA, BML and NLS.

Chapter 6

Records of birth, baptism, marriage, death and burial

These records are the ones most used by genealogists and are potentially a rich source of information since they provide us with names, dates, abodes, occupations and the proof we need to link family members together. However, such records are not without their problems, as we shall see in this chapter and the next.

An important point to bear in mind is that the churches and other religious bodies, not the civil authorities, maintained the early records. Churches were, understandably, more interested in baptisms than births, and burials rather than deaths. So when dealing with early records you might well find a baptism or burial but not a birth or death record.

The vast majority of religious records in Barbados are those maintained by the Anglican Church, which started keeping records as early as 1637. In this chapter we will focus on those records, together with civil records, which began in 1890 for births and 1925 for deaths. In the next chapter we will cover other denominational records, such as Roman Catholic, Jewish and Methodist.

Until 1855 all the Anglican Church records were kept only at parish level. However, in that year a system of central registration was introduced by act of Parliament. All the existing parish records were copied and sent to the Colonial Secretary's Office, and copies of all subsequent records were sent there each year. These centrally held church records (known as parochial registers), together with the civil records introduced in 1890 (births) and 1925 (deaths), form the principal body of records available to researchers. They are now held at the BDA and the Registration Department, and the following chart shows the records available to researchers and where they are located:

	Birth	Baptism	Marriage	Death	Burial
Barbados Department of Archives	–	1637 to 1930	1643 to 1930	–	1643 to 1930
Registration Department	1890 to date	–	1930 to date	1925 to date	–

We will look first at the records of birth, marriage and death held at the Registration Department, as these are the most recent and, therefore, probably the first you will need to consult. We will then look at the earlier Anglican records of baptism, marriage and burial held at the BDA.

BDA: Barbados Department of Archives; BML: Barbados Museum Library

Records of birth, marriage and death

By this stage, and by following the guidance in earlier chapters, you should have gathered all the information you can, and you will be ready to request one or two certificates. It is helpful, when you approach staff at the Registration Department for help in retrieving records, if you can give them as much information as possible about the people you are looking for. These are not easy records to access and any details gathered from family papers and relatives will make the task easier.

Contents of the records

Birth
Registration of births began in 1890 and the information given has changed slightly over time. A certificate will have columns for the following, some or all of which will be completed:
When born; name; sex; name and surname of father; name and maiden name of mother; place of residence and occupation of both parents; date registered; name and abode of informant.

Marriage
Records of marriage are held from 1930 and you should expect the following information:
Place and date of marriage; names and ages of both parties and their marital status (e.g. spinster, widow); occupation and abode of both; names and occupations of their fathers; and names of two witnesses.

Death
Registration of death began in 1925 and the information recorded is:
Name; age; marital status; date of death; place of death; sex; and date of registration.
The cause of death is not included on death certificates but will be provided on a separate "cause of death" certificate if requested.

Searching the records and obtaining certificates

These records have not been transcribed and made available on the Internet or in published form, so there are no shortcuts, as there are for some other records. The only option is to contact the Registration Department, and the procedure for this is described here.

If you are based outside Barbados you should write, fax or phone (no email is available); see the "List of archives" chapter for contact information. Local researchers must visit the Registration Department in person. The recommended time for this is after 2.30 p.m. since the office is usually less busy in the afternoons.

A staff member will conduct a brief search of the records held on computer, and you should provide as much of the following information as possible:

Birth
The person's name, date of birth, names of parents and parish of birth.

Marriage
The names of both parties, date of marriage, parish and place of marriage.

Death
The name of the deceased, date and place of death.

If the "event" is found, you will be told the cost for a certificate, and when payment has been made the certificate will be posted or held for you to collect. If a certificate is requested and paid for before 9.30 a.m. it can be collected after 2.30 p.m. the same day (depending on staffing levels). Otherwise it can be collected the next day. Local researchers must collect in person.

The cost of certificates is currently as follows: birth B$1, death B$5, cause of death B$10, marriage B$10 if at least one party was a citizen of Barbados or B$20 if neither party was a citizen.

If a member of staff has been unable to trace the event, you may wish to search the records yourself. This is possible but not an easy task for a number of reasons.

There is no separate search room so researchers have to work at a desk (assuming one is available) in the office where staff are dealing with members of the public who have come in to register events. The computer records are not available for public perusal so the index books must be used. There is a charge of B$5 per index covering one year. One book may be consulted at a time, and this must be paid for and a receipt obtained from the cashier in another part of the building before the book will be produced. If the event is found the full record can be consulted for B$20, following the same procedure.

The indexes for birth and death are organized by registration district, as follows:

A   St Michael
B   Christ Church and St George
C   St Philip and St John
D   St Thomas and St James
E   St Lucy and St Peter
F   St Andrew and St Joseph

The marriage records are organized by parish and are listed under the surnames of both parties. So it is always helpful to know which parish you are looking for, but since all parishes for one year are contained in the same book it is not a long job to search them all.

Births can be confusing since up to about 1970 they are listed by the name of the parent or parents rather than the child's name. So if you know the child's name but not the names of the parent/parents you will not be able to use these records. An alternative is the baptism records, which are indexed under the child's name. These are held in the same office and can be seen by the public.

There are a number of reasons why you might be unsuccessful in finding the person you are looking for, and we will discuss these at the end of this chapter.

Church records of baptism, marriage and burial

The BDA holds records of baptism, marriage and burial from the earliest times through to 1930. These are copies, made in 1855 and annually since then, of the Anglican Church records. The following table is a rough guide to the earliest records available for each parish. As this shows, coverage varies enormously from parish to parish. St Andrew in particular can be a problem area for the researcher. There are gap years for all parishes caused by damage from hurricanes, floods, fires, records being kept in poor conditions and other causes. We will discuss some of these gaps later in this chapter.

Parish	Baptisms	Marriages	Burials
Christ Church	1637	1643	1643
St Philip	1648	1672/3	1673
St Michael	1648/9	1648/9	1648/9
St James	1693	1693	1693
St Joseph	1718	1717/8	1717/8
St Thomas	1728	1723	1723
St Lucy	1747	1749	1748
St Peter	1779 (not 1825–1834)	1779	1779
St George	1801	1801	1801
St John	1805 (imperfect before 1825)	1657	1657
St Andrew	1825	1825	1825

The contents of the registers vary over the centuries, and we will look at what information you can hope to find. Some of the records are available on the Internet and in various publications and these are described here, together with guidance on using the records at the BDA.

When research of baptism, marriage and burial records goes well, it can be very satisfying. Some luck is needed, however, and we will consider some of the problems you may encounter.

Contents of Records

In the early days there were no printed forms for the parish registers and in most cases clergymen recorded the minimum details needed, though some took the opportunity to add extra snippets. In 1825 a printed form was introduced, followed by a more detailed one in 1855.

We will look at what you can expect to find when searching the parish registers.

Baptism 1637–1825
The earliest surviving baptism record (below) is typical of early records. Often, as in the registers in England at this time, the mother's name was not provided.

Christ Church – Baptism
__March 1637
Arthur son of John & Mary Spencer
BDA Ref: RL1/17/1

(_ indicates that the date is missing or illegible)

If you're lucky the clergyman will have provided extra information and, as these examples show, people being baptized were not always babies:

Christ Church – Baptism
8 May 1681
Ann aged 7 yrs, Christopher 5 yrs, Maria 2 yrs chn of Thomas & Elizabeth Mason
BDA Ref: RL1/17/117

Christ Church – Baptism
_ April 1728
Nathaniel Clarke, a man, formerly a Quaker
Mary Clarke, a woman, formerly a Quaker
Agnes Clarke, a woman, formerly a Quaker
BDA Ref: RL1/17/212

St Philip – Baptism
4 Apr 1788
William, Peter, Samuel, Joseph, Esther, Ann, Mariah & Henrietta free black chn of Ann Padmore free Negro
BDA Ref: RL1/22/203

Illegitimacy was common in the early days and here are some ways in which the fact was recorded in baptism records:

St Thomas – Baptism
2 Apr 1757
William & Henry bastards of William Smithwick & Sarah Chadderton
BDA Ref: RL1/49/52

NLS: National Library Service; JBMHS: Journal of the Barbados Museum & Historical Society

St James – Baptism
6 Aug 1775
Rebecca Ann the base b. dau of Elizabeth Devin
BDA Ref: RL1/46/457

Baptism 1825–1855

In 1825 the first printed form was introduced, and this asked for the date of baptism, name, parents' names, abode and quality, trade or profession of father. This is an example of a very helpful entry and is a reminder that these records are handwritten copies of the originals and, therefore, subject to error. Is the child really Wolf, or maybe Rolf?

Christ Church – Baptism
29 Jan 1826
Wolf Harrison
Parents: Alexander & Mary McDonald
Abode: Oistins Fort
Occupation of father: soldier in the 25th Regiment
BDA Ref: RL1/17/433

Baptism after 1855

The new form introduced at this time added the date of birth and mother's maiden name:

St George – Baptism
Baptism date: 25 Mar 1875
Birth date: 8 Jan 1875
Julia Eglantine King
Parents: Samuel & Sarah Elizabeth King
Mother's maiden name: Prout
Abode: Prout's Village
Occupation of father: domestic
Minister officiating: WC Watson
BDA Ref: RL2/62/370

Marriage 1643–1825

The earliest marriage documented in the records was in 1643, and the details recorded before 1825 rarely went beyond the basics, as shown below. Occasionally mention was made of marital status—widowed or spinster for example.

Christ Church – Marriage
9 Apr 1643
Joseph Gardner & Jane Page
BDA Ref: RL1/20/1

BDA: Barbados Department of Archives; BML: Barbados Museum Library

The following Christ Church marriage ties in neatly with the baptism in 1681 listed above:
Christ Church – Marriage
14 Jan 1674
Thomas Mason & Elizabeth Lambert
BDA Ref: RL1/20/58

An example of a marriage providing useful extra information:

St Michael – Marriage
27 May 1818
Jeremiah Gosling, (63rd Regiment)
Mary Ann Taylor
BDA Ref: RL1/7/103

Marriage 1825–1855
The printed form introduced for marriages in 1825 required the date, names and parish of residence of both parties, whether married by banns or license, plus the names of two witnesses. Here is an example showing this information:

Christ Church – Marriage
30 Jun 1833
John Edward Kennedy of Christ Church
Mary Ann Nurse of Christ Church
By banns
Officiating Minister: J.H. Orderson
Witnesses: Thomas L. Ruck, James Alleyne Nurse
BDA ref: RL1/20/200

Marriage after 1855
The new form introduced in 1855 added (for both parties) age, condition (i.e., marital status), occupation, residence, names and occupations of their fathers. Where all questions have been answered these records are a gift for genealogists, as this example illustrates:

St Michael, Chapel of St Stephen – Marriage
22 Sept 1855
Samuel Thomas Graham aged 40 years, widower, labourer of Seals Lane
Father: Shadrock Graham, labourer
Amelia Crick aged 25 years, spinster, labourer of Seals Lane
Father: Tobias Crick, butcher
Officiating minister: William Gill
Witness: Tobias Crick
BDA Ref: RL1/18/236

As you can see, the two witnesses requirement was not always met.

Burial 1643–1825
Like the other records, burials had minimal information to start with, with the odd exception. Where appropriate the description "child" was added. The oldest burial record (1643) is shown here along with some examples that give additional, useful information.

Christ Church – Burial
__ April 1643
Paul Crichlow
BDA Ref: RL1/21/1

Christ Church – Burial
25 Feb 1644
Philly James servant to Capt Middleton
BDA Ref: RL1/21/1

St George – Burial
30 Jun 1801
John Prettyjohn aged 72, died 29 Jun, was buried in St George's Church
BDA Ref: RL1/56/9

Burial 1825–1855
The form introduced at this time called for the name, age and abode of the deceased and date of burial. The addition of a small amount of information can add greatly to our knowledge of a person at a certain time. Compare this burial record with the marriage of the same man in 1818 given on page 25:

St Michael – Burial
9 June 1841
Jeremiah Gosling aged 55, pauper
Abode: Bridgetown Alms House
Officiating minister: no service, Thomas Clarke, curate
BDA Ref: RL1/16/234

Burial after 1855
The new form used from this date added the deceased's place of birth and occupation.

The place of birth was often stated as "Barbados," as this St Thomas example shows, and this does not help us much:

St Thomas – Burial
16 Mar 1859
Mary Ann Jones aged 15 years
daughter of carpenter
Abode: Canefield
Place of birth: Barbados
BDA Ref: RL2/29/640

This St George record is much more helpful:

St George – Burial
7 Mar 1859
Peggy Smart aged 65 years, labourer
Abode: near The Belle
Place of birth: Salters
BDA Ref: RL2/29/661

Free colored and slaves in the records

Reference in these records to the black population, both free and slaves, is rare in the early years. The situation changed early in the 19th century, when large numbers were baptized, married and buried by the church. Several parishes maintained separate records for their black members, and some had separate records for three different categories: slaves, apprentice laborers (during the apprentice period 1834–38) and free colored.

This marriage record is typical of the type of information recorded about slaves:

Christ Church – Marriage
21 Jun 1834
Henry Bourne, slave of Miss Norgrove
Clarissa, slave of Richard Chase
Both of this parish
Officiating minister: Christopher C Gill, Rector
Witnessed by Jeffrey Robinson
BDA Ref: RL1/20/225

Figure 3 on the following page is an example of a marriage during the apprentice period. Guy and Jubah Doll are described as "apprenticed labourers of Coverley Estate."

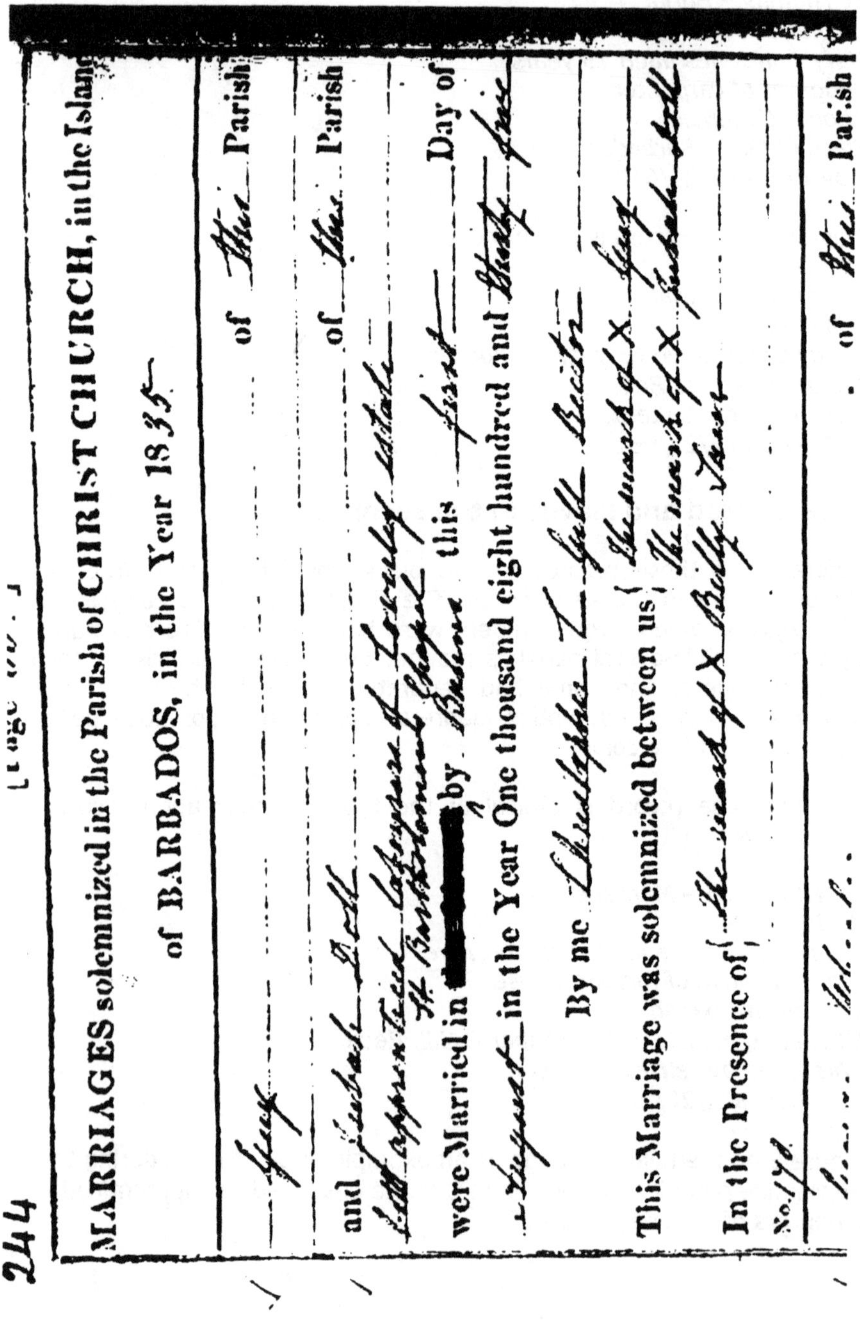

Figure 3   1835 marriage of apprenticed laborers (BDA Ref: RL1/20/244)

The following tables indicate the separate parish records that have been identified for black members of the parish. The BDA references given will help you trace individual entries.

Baptism records

Parish	BDA reference	Free colored	Slave	Apprentice
Christ Church	RL1/17/533–643		Jan 1822–Jul 1834	
St George	RL1/52/222–468		Jan 1826–Aug 1834	Aug 1834
St Lucy	RL1/36/295–358	Sep 1821–Dec 1832	Jan 1833–Jul 1834	Aug 1834–Jul 1838
St James	RL1/46/806–870	Apr 1793–Dec 1825		
St James	RL1/48		Dec 1825–Jul 1834	
St John	RL1/26/351–556		Mar 1832–Jul 1834	Aug 1834–Feb 1835
St Joseph	RL1/30	1816–May 1825	1816–Jul 1834	
St Michael	RL1/7/534–586		Jul 1823–Jun 1827	
St Peter	RL1/39/188–258		Oct 1825–Jul 1834	
St Philip	RL1/22/352–492		1824–Aug 1834	
St Thomas	RL1/49	Dec 1811–Feb 1824	Jan 1824–Jan 1825 & Jan 1829–May 1833	
St Thomas	RL1/50		May 1833–Jul 1834	

Marriage Records

Parish	BDA reference	Free colored	Slave	Apprentice
Christ Church	RL1/20		Jun 1826– Oct 1832	
St George	RL1/55		Jan 1827– Aug 1834	
St James	RL1/46/806– 870	Apr 1793– Dec 1825	-	
St Thomas	RL1/49		Sep 1828– Jul 1834	

Burial Records

Parish	BDA reference	Free colored	Slave	Apprentice
Christ Church	RL1/21/207– 214		Feb1824– Aug 1834	
St George	RL1/56/100– 112		Nov 1825– Aug 1834	
St Lucy	RL1/38/616– 626	Dec 1816– Jun 1834		Aug 1834– Jul 1838
St James	RL1/46/806– 870	Apr 1793– Dec 1825		
St James	RL1/48		Mar 1826– Oct 1833	
St Joseph	RL1/32	1820– 1824	1820–1824	
St Peter	RL1/39		Oct 1825– Apr 1834	
St Philip	RL1/25/457– 461		Mar 1825– Aug 1833	
St Thomas	RL1/49	Dec 1811– Feb 1824	Jan 1825– Aug 1834	

A note about dates

Dates in parish registers before 1752 can be confusing. Until that year the old-style Julian calendar was used whereby the year began on Lady Day, 25 March. So, for example, 31 December 1700 was followed by 1 January 1700. The year didn't change until 25 March 1701, the day following 24 March 1700.

When the Barbados parish registers were called in and copied in 1855 the copiers sometimes made an adjustment, but there was no uniformity in this. Some records show a year change on 1 January. Others describe the months January to 24 March as, for example, 1700/1701 (known as "double dating"). Others show the year changing on 25 March—old style.

The Gregorian calendar (January to December) was introduced on 1 January 1752. If you are consulting a record in the first quarter of a year before 1752, it is worth checking back to January to see what change if any was made in the copied record.

To add further confusion, the dates between 2 and 14 September 1752 were cancelled altogether! This was to allow England (and its colonies) to catch up with Europe, which had changed to the Gregorian calendar earlier; the absence of leap years in the Julian calendar had caused England to fall behind.

Searching the records

Before you head for the BDA to look at the records, bear in mind several other sources that are available to you. You could save time by checking these first.

The International Genealogical Index (IGI)
The Church of Jesus Christ of Latter-day Saints (the Mormons) has filmed parish registers all over the world and brought them together in their IGI. Records of baptism and marriage (not generally burial) for Barbados up to about 1880 are included and can be seen on the LDS website **www.familysearch.org**.

A search can be carried out by surname and specifying "Barbados." All records for that surname will be listed. Simply click on any events of interest and more details will be brought up. As an index, it will give only the basic details. Here, for example, is the entry for a marriage we looked at earlier:

Marriage: 22 Sep 1855, St Michael, Samuel Thos. Graham and Amelia Crick.

In common with all indexes based on old records, there are errors and omissions. If you don't find what you are looking for it is still worth checking the records held at the BDA.

Another way to access the IGI is on microfiche at the BDA. This material is freely available in the microfilm and microfiche reading room adjacent to the search room. The microfiches are organized alphabetically by surname.

LDS Family History Centers
If you are based outside Barbados it is still possible for you to access the records of baptism, marriage and burial by visiting one of the Family History Centers located in the meetinghouses of the Church of Jesus Christ of Latter-day Saints. There are more than 3,400 of these worldwide, administered and operated by local church members. Microfilms can be borrowed from the LDS main library in Salt Lake City for a small fee and delivered to a local center for you to access. The library holds records on microfilm for baptism, marriage, burial and birth in Barbados up to 1930. See **www.familysearch.org** for more information on the centers and library holdings.

Sanders, Joanne McRee. *Barbados Records: Baptisms 1637–1800*
Sanders, Joanne McRee. *Barbados Records: Marriages 1643–1800* (2 volumes)
(BDA, BML, NLS)
These invaluable publications were compiled by Mrs McRee Sanders from the records held at the BDA. Records of baptism 1637–1800 and marriages 1643–1800 have been extracted and the entries are listed in full. There are no entries for St George and St Andrew, since surviving records for those parishes do not start until 1801 and 1825 respectively. For St John, baptisms are not included because the surviving records start in 1825. The records are arranged by parish and then by date, and there is an index of surnames. The foreword for each parish is worth reading for its notes on the records. The work is now also available on CD-ROM.

Burial records on the Internet

Burial records for some parishes, particularly St Joseph, have been transcribed and included on **www.tombstones.bb**. This is an ongoing project by Ms Lisa Jenkins of New Jersey and currently includes:

- St Joseph 1718–1849 (there is a gap in the records of 23 years from 25 April 1727–20 November 1750)
- Some entries for St John parish from 1657 to 1848, although this is not a complete listing

Ms Jenkins notes gaps of about 57 years in the St John burial register, as follows:

- 27 Feb 1669–7 Sep 1684
- All of 1708
- 26 Nov 1722–21 Apr 1733
- 21 Dec 1766–22 Jan 1771
- 24 Nov 1783–beginning of 1789
- 17 Oct 1800–4 Sep 1825

A search can be made for a specific name, or the entire register can be scanned. This website is covered in more detail in the "Gravestones and cemetery records" chapter.

Hotten, J.C. *Original Lists of Persons of Quality...and Others Who Went from Great Britain to the American Plantations, 1600–1700* (BDA, BML)
and
Brandow, James C. *Omitted Chapters from Hotten's Original List of Persons of Quality* (BDA, BML)

Records of baptism and burial are listed in these books for the period 25 March 1678 to 29 September 1679 for all parishes.

- Hotten covers baptism and burial for five of the eleven parishes: St Andrew, Christ Church, St George, St James and St Michael, plus baptisms for St John.
- Brandow covers baptism and burial for the remaining parishes: St Lucy, St Joseph, St Peter, St Philip and St Thomas, plus burials for St John.

The records were copied from returns sent by Governor Sir John Atkins to the Plantation Office in Whitehall, London, in 1679/80. The returns are now held at the National Archives in London. Although they cover only a short period these are valuable listings, as the original records for only four of the parishes have survived.

Journal of the Barbados Museum & Historical Society Vol. 27

Similar returns are held in London for the years 1715/16, and the records were copied by R.V. Taylor for the *Journal*. Mr Taylor concentrated on those parishes for which the records are missing.

Unfortunately St Thomas and St Lucy were not included, though their records too are now missing. Those included are:

- Baptism and burial: 25 Apr 1715–24 Apr 1716 for St Andrew, St George and St Peter
- Baptism only 25 Apr 1715–24 Apr 1716 for St John
- Baptism: 29 Oct 1715–23 Jul 1716 for St Joseph
- Burial: 13 Nov 1715–18 Jun 1716 for St Joseph

The IGI and other finding aids described above offer useful shortcuts for research but remember they are all copies. Whenever a record is copied there is the potential for error, so it is always advisable to check the original source records.

Consulting the records at the Barbados Department of Archives

The BDA holds indexes for all its records of baptism, marriage and burial and, like the records themselves, the indexes are available on microfilm.

Records are indexed by year. Within each year surnames are listed alphabetically and grouped together by parish. Reference numbers next to each person's name refer to the volume and page number where the church record can be found. To request an index you should refer to the chart found on each table in the BDA search room. Listed under baptism, marriage and burial, these will tell you the reference number for the year(s) you are interested in.

We will look at an example relating to the Grogan and Chase families of Christ Church parish. Our research has taken us as far as this baptism record for William Chase in 1840:

Chapel of St Lawrence, Christ Church – Baptism
4 Feb 1840
William Chase son of Edward & Elizabeth Mary Grogan
Abode: Roadside
Profession / occupation of parent: planter
BDA Ref: RL1/18/666

The next step is to look for a marriage for William's parents. We have the names of the bride and groom and a year in which to start our search. The chart on the search room table tells us that index RL1/67 covers the years 1839–1848 and index RL1/66 covers 1769–1838. We can now request these microfilms, noting that we are searching for the letter G.

A search working back from the year of birth reveals a marriage in 1835, so we note down the references given:

- Year: 1835
- Parish: Christ Church
- Name: Edward Grogan
- Volume number: 20
- Page number: 248

We now have enough information to request the next microfilm from a member of staff. The records of baptism, marriage and burial all have the prefix RL1 until 1848 and RL3 from 1849. So we must request RL1/20. When the microfilm is delivered we can turn straight to page 248 to find our entry:

Christ Church parish church – Marriage
27 Oct 1835
Edward Grogan junior to Elizabeth Mary Chase
Witnesses: Robert C Chase & B Grogan
RL1/20/248

When using these records be sure to note the church or chapel where the event took place. This information may be on a previous page and can easily be overlooked.

It is not always so easy to find what you are looking for. For the more common surnames there may be many entries in the index. It can then be a long task to check all the references for the relevant ones. If you have a number of surnames of interest, it is worth starting with the less common ones while you build up your skills and find your way round the records.

Try using the worksheets included in Appendix 2. They can be photo-copied and enlarged to a more workable size, giving you plenty of space to record all the bits of vital information you need.

Obtaining copies of certificates of baptism, marriage and burial

It is not possible to obtain photocopies, digital scans or other "images" of these records in Barbados. Copies are handwritten onto a certificate by a member of staff and will include only information found in the church records. In many cases they have less information, as the extra details added by church ministers in the earlier records will not be included. For family history purposes the information extracted from the records is usually sufficient, and there is no need to obtain copies of certificates.

If you do, exceptionally, wish to order a certificate, these are issued by the Registration Department; the BDA is not able to issue them. There is no charge for baptism or burial certificates. The cost of a marriage certificate is currently B$10 if at least one party was a resident of Barbados or B$20 if neither party was a resident. Postage is payable on all certificates mailed abroad. Certificates of baptism are not issued beyond 1890, the year in which birth registration began. Burial certificates are issued until 1925 when death registration began. The Registration Department will require the BDA reference number and all the information contained in the original record. The procedure to be followed for ordering a certificate is the same as that described earlier for birth, marriage and death records.

Possible problems

When research in the parish registers goes well and generations of a family fit neatly together it can be very satisfying. However most of us come to a dead end at some point, and there are numerous reasons for this; we will look at some of these here. In some cases it is just not possible to progress the research further. Here are some common problems encountered:

> Illiteracy was very common in the past and surnames were written in the register as they were heard. You may be a Clark without an e but almost certainly your ancestors will have been recorded as Clarke as well as Clark. A Goslin will have been Gosling, Gossling and Gosslin. Look out for short forms of names too. Williams may be Wms and Richards Richds.

> On the subject of names, remember that Christian or first names were often passed down in families. This can help to tie in an individual to a particular family.

> Some people were married and buried under different names from their baptismal ones, possibly their second name or some completely different name.

> You may have found a burial or marriage record giving a person's age, and this does not tally with their date of birth as shown in the baptism record. Death records in particular often have wrong ages, since the information was provided by the person registering the death, who may not have been close to the deceased and had to take a guess. Guesses are often rounded up to the nearest 5 or 0 so watch out for 80, 85, etc. The elderly are sometimes known for exaggerating their age (in both directions!) and this may cause errors. On marriage some women marrying a younger man may

reduce their age slightly or a young groom may exaggerate his age. Often in the past people simply did not know their exact age. So approach these numbers with caution.

> A common problem is the lack of fathers' names in the baptism records. If you come across this you are not alone. A sample month, July 1859, was checked in the Chapel of St Luke in the parish of St George. Of the 12 baptisms recorded, only 4 named the father. In some cases these children later took their father's name or another surname, and this name may appear on their marriage or burial certificates. The Barbadian historian Dr Pedro Welch encountered these problems in his own family research and overcame them to trace his family back to a slave ancestor born about 1812. You can see his family history on **www.mahaica.net**.

> Where the parents did marry, remember that many children were born before marriage or within a short time of the ceremony, so be flexible in the time period you search.

> You may find baptism records for the children of a married couple, but no marriage. There was much traveling back and forth of the wealthier families, and marriages, baptisms and burials took place in both Barbados and England (as well as other places). The IGI can be helpful with this as it includes records for other countries. Also, newspaper announcements sometimes recorded events abroad for prominent citizens—see the "Newspapers and directories" chapter.

> Burials during epidemics often went unrecorded.

> Many children died in infancy. If you have a baptism but no further mention of the person, try the burials register.

> People being baptized were not always babies; baptism of two or more brothers and sisters sometimes took place on the same day. Two children baptized together are not necessarily twins.

> A lack of any baptism, marriage or burials in the records could indicate that your ancestors were non-conformists; see the next chapter.

> There are some separate records for the St Ann's Garrison with their own indexes. If your ancestor was a soldier, see the "Military records" chapter.

By far the commonest problem encountered by researchers is the lack of records for the period in question. As mentioned before, the tropical climate has taken its toll, and records were not always given the care they needed. There are many gaps of whole weeks or even years, and even where records do exist there may be holes in the pages depriving us of some facts

Mrs McRee Sanders, in her *Barbados Records* described on page 32, gives a detailed analysis of the baptism and marriage records she copied. Appendix 3 gives a list of the gaps she found. Please note that no such analysis has been carried out of the burial records, except those described above for St Joseph and St John on the website **www.tombstones.bb**. Also bear in mind that the information in *Barbados Records* and Appendix 3 relates only to records up to 1800.

Finally it should be remembered that the records of baptism, marriage and burial we have access to are in fact copies of the originals. As with all copies, human error comes in and there are sure to be some mistakes.

Chapter 7

Catholic, Jewish and non-conformist records

Soon after settlement in 1627 a Jewish community was established in Barbados, and over the next two hundred years Quakers, Catholics, Methodists and Moravians arrived and settled on the island. We will look at the records and other sources for each of these.

This chart shows the starting date of records held at the BDA.

	Birth	Baptism	Marriage	Death	Burial
Catholic		1839	1839		1847
Methodist		1826	1830		1854
Moravian		1768	1827		1768
Jewish	1779		1811	1660	
Quaker	No records survive				

The procedure for searching these records is the same as for the Anglican Church, as described in the previous chapter. From 1886 all denominations are indexed together, but for the years up to 1885 there is a separate index for "other denominations."

The index references up to 1885 are:

Baptism RL1/84
Marriage RL1/85
Burial RL1/86

Note that this group of records is *not* included in the LDS Church IGI and its website.

Catholics

A Roman Catholic mission was established in Barbados in 1839 and the St Patrick's Cathedral was opened in 1848. Four more churches were built later in Black Rock, Maxwell, St James and St John.

There are baptism and marriage records from 1839 and burials from 1847, and they follow the same format as those for the Anglican Church described in the previous chapter.

Many of the early Catholic records relate to the St Ann's Garrison as Figure 4 shows. These two marriages in 1841 were officiated over by W Rogers, minister to HM Troops.

Further reading

Shorrocks, Rev. Francis. *History of the Catholic Church in Barbados During the 19th Century,* JBMHS 25: 102–122.

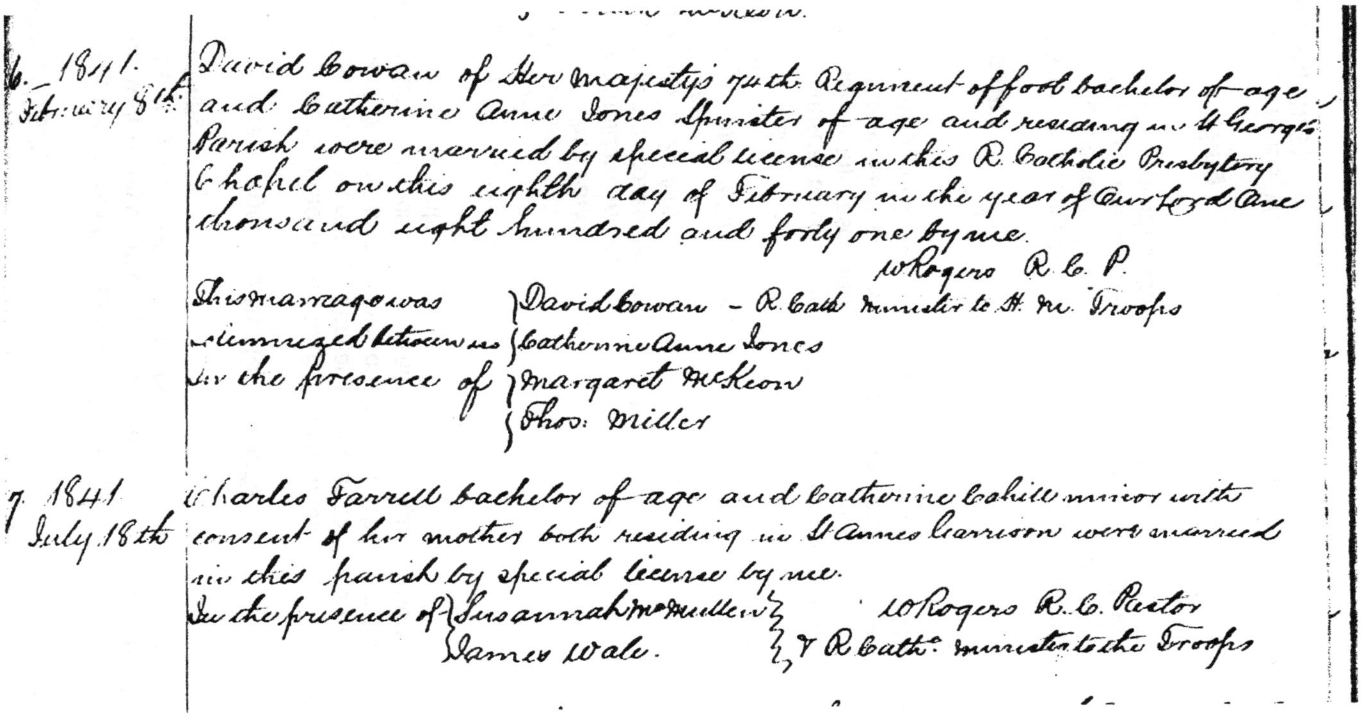

6. 1841. February 8th. David Cowan of Her Majesty's 74th Regiment of foot bachelor of age and Catherine Anne Jones Spinster of age and residing in St George's Parish were married by special license in this R. Catholic Presbytery Chapel on this eighth day of February in the year of Our Lord One thousand eight hundred and forty one by me.

W Rogers R. C. P.

This marriage was solemnized between us } David Cowan – R. Cath minister to H. M. Troops
} Catherine Anne Jones
in the presence of } Margaret McKeon
} Thos: Miller

7. 1841 July 18th Charles Farrell bachelor of age and Catherine Cahill minor with consent of her mother both residing in St Annes Garrison were married in this parish by special license by me.

In the presence of { Susannah McMullen } W Rogers R. C. Rector
James Wale. } & R Cath. minister to the Troops

Figure 4 1841 Roman Catholic marriage (BDA Ref: RL1/73/323)

Methodists

Methodists first arrived in Barbados in the late 18th century but they were not well received initially. A second attempt was made, and by the 1820s they had established themselves and went on to have a large following.

Baptism, marriage and burial records

There are baptism records from 1826, marriages from 1830 and burials from 1854. The records are similar in format to those for the Anglican Church and printed forms were often used. This was not always the case though, and below is an example of a burial where the minister chose to give extra information.

Bethel Methodist Church – Burial
22 May 1854
Susannah Walker
Residence: White Park
Trade or condition: widow
Cause of death: consumption
Date of death: 20 May 1854
Age: 65 years
Officiating minister: Tilney Rising
RL1/77/8

It is very unusual to come across "cause of death" in a parish register, and it makes for fascinating reading. Some of the more common causes in 1854 were dropsy, severe cramp and cholera (this was an epidemic year), and cold was common among babies and young children.

Other sources

The NLS holds a collection on microfilm of Methodist church records covering the period 1767–1948, including minute books, accounts, reports, diaries, miscellaneous documents and church books for Barbados and some other Caribbean territories.

Further reading

Blackman, Francis W. (Woodie). *Methodism: 200 Years in Barbados* (BDA, BML, NLS)

BDA: Barbados Department of Archives; BML: Barbados Museum Library

Titus, Noel F. *The Development of Methodism in Barbados 1823–1883* (BDA, NLS)

Moravians

Moravian missionary work began in Barbados in 1765. According to Aldersley (below) theirs was "the first successful attempt by any church to carry the Gospel of the Lord Jesus Christ to the unfortunate slaves of the West Indies."

The format of Moravian records is quite different from those kept by the Anglican and other churches. This is a reflection of their role as missionaries, and most records before emancipation relate to slaves.

Baptism/burial records from 1768

The baptism/burial records serve as a lifetime record of members of the church, with only marriage being recorded separately. There are separate records kept for men, women, boys, girls and children of missionaries. The following are typical of the format for the early records of baptism/burial.

The records for men and women have columns headed: baptismal name, former name, owner or plantation, nation (often left blank, typical answer—creole), by whom baptized, date of baptism or date of reception into the congregation, admission to the communion, moved or sold from the island, departed this life, place of burial.

This example from the Sharon Moravian Church register relating to a boy illustrates the slightly different format in the children's registers:

Name: David
Place of birth: Blowers
By whom baptized: Jno N. Ganson
Date of baptism: 2 Sep 1810
Father & Mother: Flora, Joe
Owner or plantation: Blowers
Departed this life: 9 Nov 1812
Place of burial: on the estate
RL1/73/123

Separate registers were kept for children of missionaries and include the following information: name, parents, date of birth, date of baptism, name of officiating minister, sponsors, departed this life and where buried.

Following emancipation the format used for children of missionaries became the norm for all members of the church.

Marriage records from 1827

These are more conventional and include typically: date, names of both parties, age, condition (widowed, spinster, etc), rank or profession, residence, whether married by license or banns, consent by whom given (in the case of minors), names of 2 witnesses and the name of the officiating minister.

Other sources

Some other records relating to the Sharon, Mount Tabor and Clifton Hill churches are held on microfilm at the BDA and NLS. In addition to church books of baptism, marriage and burial they include Sunday school registers, missionaries' diaries and various other documents.

Further reading

Aldersley, Cyril F. *The Moravians, Two Centuries of Work in Barbados* (BDA)

Lewis, K. *The Moravian Mission in Barbados, 1816–1886: A Study of the Historical Context and Theological Significance of a Minority Church Among an Oppressed People* (BDA, BML, NLS)

The Moravian Mission in Barbados: Historical Sketch of the Past 100 Years, (Extracted from The Barbados Times, May 1865) JBMHS 31:73–78 (BDA, BML, NLS)

Jews

Soon after settlement a Jewish community was established in Barbados and by 1679 it had 300 members.

The Jewish records held at the BDA relate to birth rather than baptism, and death rather than burial. Dates are given in both Hebrew and English.

Birth from 1779

Records include only the child's name and those of the parents. These records are quite difficult to decipher and although they cover many years, the number of entries is relatively small.

BDA: Barbados Department of Archives; BML: Barbados Museum Library

Marriage from 1811

The couple is named, and later entries include the names of parents. Again, these are not easy to read. Although they cover 60 years, only 29 marriages are recorded.

Death from 1660

The name of the deceased is given and sometimes age and relationship (e.g., wife of, husband of).

Many of the people in this register are buried in the Jewish Synagogue burial ground in Bridgetown and are included in E.M. Shilstone's book mentioned below. The book has appendices listing those in the death register for whom there is no memorial in the graveyard.

Other sources

The BML holds a large collection of information on the Jews of Barbados. This is gathered together in a folder and includes many names of individuals. Notebooks containing Jewish information can also be found in the BML's Shilstone Collection.

Jews resident in Bridgetown in 1679–80 were listed separately in the census for that period. See the "Census records" chapter for more information.

Shilstone, Eustace M. *Monumental Inscriptions in the Burial Ground of the Jewish Synagogue at Bridgetown, Barbados* **(BDA, BML, NLS)**
Contains 374 epitaphs in the original Hebrew with English translation.

www.jewishgen.org/cemetery/atl-caribbean/barbados.html
This website is of interest for Jewish genealogy relating to Barbados and has links to other related sites.

www.tombstones.bb
The English translations of the epitaphs from the Jewish Synagogue Burial Ground, transcribed by E.M. Shilstone (see above), are included here.

Further reading

American Jewish Historical Society Publications (BDA)

Arbell, Mordechai. *The Jewish Nation of the Caribbean*

Farrar, Rev. Canon P.A. *The Jews in Barbados,* JBMHS 9: 130–133 (BDA, BML, NLS)

Schreuder, Yda. *A True Global Community: Sephardic Jews, the Sugar Trade and Barbados in the Seventeenth Century,* JBMHS 50: 166–194 (BDA, BML, NLS)

Shilstone, E.M. *The Jewish Synagogue Bridgetown, Barbados,* JBMHS 32: 3–15 (BDA, BML, NLS)

Watson, Karl. *The Iconography of Tombstones in the Jewish Graveyard, Bridgetown, Barbados,* JBMHS 50: 195–212 (BDA, BML, NLS)

Welch, Pedro L.V. *Jews in a Caribbean Colonial Society: Resistance and Accommodation in Bridgetown, Barbados, 1675–1834,* JBMHS 44: 54–64 (BDA, BML, NLS)

Quakers (The Religious Society of Friends)

In 1655, within eight years of George Fox beginning his Quaker ministry in England, the doctrine was brought to Barbados. By 1659 several meetings had been formed and many influential people had adopted the Quaker principles. From the start life was made difficult for the Friends, and by the early 19th century there were very few left on the island.

Since Quakers refused to conform to the Anglican Church, they were generally not recorded in the parish registers. They established their own registration system for birth, marriage and burial. These records do not survive in Barbados. For any Friends who were born and married in England before settling in Barbados, there is likely to be a record of their birth (assuming they were a birthright Quaker) and marriage in the Digest Registers of Quaker births, marriages and burials. These cover approximately 1650–1837, when civil registration was introduced in England. There is a summary of the Digest Registers on the website of the Quaker Library in London: **www.quaker.org.uk/library/guides/libgenea.html**

Other sources

Besse, Joseph. *Sufferings of Early Quakers, America—New England & Maryland, West Indies—Antigua Barbados Jamaica and Nevis, Bermuda* (BDA, BML)
Quakers suffered persecution for their beliefs for many years. For example, they were often fined or imprisoned for refusing to take oaths, serve in the armed forces or support the Anglican Church by paying tithes. Cases of persecution were recorded in books of sufferings, and in 1753 Joseph Besse published a detailed account of those occurring in Barbados, among other places. This has now been reprinted with a new introduction and an index of people and places. More than 70 pages of the book relate to Barbados, and this is a rich source of information on Barbados Quakers.

Sources at the BML
The BML holds a large collection of information on the Quakers of Barbados. This is gathered together in a folder and includes many names of individuals. Notebooks containing Quaker information can also be found in the Library's Shilstone Collection.

The Journal of the Barbados Museum and Historical Society (BDA, BML, NLS)
The Journal has published numerous articles on Quakers, many of them listing names:

Brinegar, L. Brett. *Radical Politics and Civil Disobedience: Quaker Resistance in Seventeenth Century Bridgetown,*
Vol. 49: 150–166

Brome, Joseph A. (Ed. by) *John Candlers Visit to Barbados 1849,*
Vol. 28: 128–136

Cadbury, Henry J. *Barbados Quakers 1683–1761, Preliminary List,*
Vol. 9: 29–31*

Cadbury, Henry J. *Account of Barbados 200 Years Ago,*
Vol. 9: 81–83

Cadbury, Henry J. *186 Barbados ʻQuakeresses in 1677,*
Vol. 9: 195–197 *

Cadbury, Henry J. *A Quaker Account of Barbados in 1718,*
Vol. 10: 118–124

Cadbury, Henry J. *Witnesses of a Quaker marriage in 1689,*
Vol. 14: 186–187 *

Cadbury, Henry J. *Glimpses of Barbados Quakerism 1676–79,*
Vol. 20: 67–70

Cadbury, Henry J. *Quakers in Barbados in 1687,* Vol. 34: 53–57 *

Dailey, Barbara Ritter. *The Early Quaker Mission and the Settlement of Meetings in Barbados, 1655–1700,* Vol. 39: 24–46

Durham, Harriet Frorer. *Laws of Barbados Directed at Quakers, 1676–1723,* Vol. 34: 73–75

Gragg, Larry Dale. *The Making of an Abolitionist: Benjamin Lay on Barbados, 1718–1720,* Vol. 47: 166–184

Pearce, Clifford. *The Quaker Property in Barbados,* Vol. 35: 287–299

Shilstone E.M. *Some Early Records of the Friends in Barbados,* Vol. 34: 43–52

* Repeated in Brandow's *Genealogies of Barbados Families*

The Committee for Preservation of the Quaker Burial Ground at The Cliff, opposite St Philip Church.
Four main Quaker burial grounds are known to have existed in Barbados as well as a few on plantations. The one in St Philip is the only one to have been restored. Details of surviving monumental inscriptions can be found at **www.tombstones.bb**.

Further reading

Durham, Harriet Frorer. *Caribbean Quakers* (BDA, BML)

Chapter 8

Census records and other lists of people

The sources described in this chapter mainly relate to the white landowning section of society in pre-emancipation times. For those researching colonists who moved from Barbados to North America, these lists can be particularly helpful as they may give some clue to people's origin. In some cases the original records are in London, but published transcriptions are available and these are described here. The most important publications for this group of records are:

Hotten, J.C. *Original Lists of Persons of Quality...and Others Who Went from Great Britain to the American Plantations, 1600–1700* (BDA, BML)

Brandow, James C. *Omitted Chapters from Hotten's Original List of Persons of Quality* (BDA, BML)

Kent, D.L. *Barbados & America* (BDA, BML, NLS)

Census records

Census records are a good source for family historians as they place people in a location at a particular time often with ages, family groupings and other helpful information. For Barbados there are two good early examples: those for 1679/80 and 1715. Both were provided by the Island's Governor at the request of the Plantation Office in Whitehall, London. The originals are held in London at the National Archives (formerly the Public Record Office).

Unfortunately no later census records of interest to family historians are available.

1679/80 Census

Contents
Organized by parish, the names of 2,639 landholders are listed along with the number of acres, servants and slaves belonging to each. In addition, for Bridgetown there is a list of 405 householders showing which were married and the number of children, servants and slaves for each. There is a separate list of the 54 Jewish households in Bridgetown.

It should be remembered that the census does not list the entire population, so your ancestor may have been on the island but not eligible to be included.

Where to see the 1679/80 census
Hotten's *Original Lists* includes five of the eleven parishes: St Andrew, Christ Church, St George, St James, St Michael and the list of house-holders in Bridgetown.

Brandow's *Omitted Chapters from Hotten* and Kent's *Barbados & America*
Both include the remaining six parishes: St John, St Joseph, St Lucy, St Peter, St Philip and St Thomas.

www.rootsweb.com/~brbwgw/PubForums.htm
Names on the census are listed on this website but no additional information is given.

Further reading
For analysis of the census and an insight into life in Barbados at that time see:
Dunn, Richard S. *The Barbados Census of 1680: Profile of the Richest Colony in English America*, JBMHS 33: 57–75 (BDA, BML, NLS)

1715 Census

Contents
Like the earlier census this is a record of white inhabitants. However, a very small number described as "molata" or "of the negro extract" are included. These are children of free white women and enslaved black men. Since children took their status from their mother, they were born free and were, therefore, entitled to be listed on the census.

Unlike that of the 1679/80 census, the information given varies according to parish and in some cases entire households are named, which can be very helpful.

The parishes of St James, St Joseph, St Lucy, St Michael and St Peter give the name of the head of the household along with the number and ages of men, women, boys and girls.

The parishes of St Andrew, Christ Church, St George, St John and St Philip name all members of the household and their ages. They are bracketed together for each household.

St Thomas gives the same information but instead of being bracketed together by household, men, women and children are listed in separate groups. This makes it more difficult to identify family groups.

Where to see the 1715 census
A manuscript copy of the original 1715 census is held by the BDA. A copy can be seen on the shelves of the search room.

Data for the parishes of Christ Church, St George, St Michael and St Thomas have been copied from the above transcript and are listed in the JBMHS, Vols. 4–9.

D. L. Kent in his book *Barbados & America* gives a full listing for all parishes. The author was disturbed to find so many discrepancies between the original census in the National Archives, London and the copy held at the BDA. He made a new transcript of the census and published it in full in his book, along with a discussion of the number and kind of errors in the earlier transcript. The book includes a full name index. In the index an asterisk indicates that names relate to the 1679/80 census. All others relate to 1715.

Other lists

A small collection of lists of inhabitants is available at the BDA. The documents have been restored and are, therefore, fairly easy to use though some of the wording is difficult to read. Typically the information given is as follows: name of the master or mistress of the household along with numbers (no names) in the household under headings such as "free men and women," "men and women not free," "negro men and women," "slaves," and "men fit for bearing arms."

The surviving records with their BDA reference numbers are:
- St Thomas 1830 Ref RB9/3/1
- St George 24 March 1739/40 Ref: RB9/3/3
- Parish not named but likely Christ Church, estimated after 1758 Ref: RB9/3/4
- St John 1774 Ref: RB9/3/5
- St Peter 1780 Ref: RB9/3/6

"Names of the Inhabitants of Barbados, in the Year 1638, who then possess'd more than ten Acres of Land"

More than 700 names are listed. The list is included in Campbell, P.F., *Some Early Barbadian History* (BML, NLS)

It can also be found on the following website:
www.candoo.com/genresources/1638barbadoslist.txt.

Eminent planters in Barbados in 1673

A list of the 74 "most eminent" planters was sent to the Colonial Office in London in 1673. These are the big landowners with holdings ranging from 200 to 1,000 acres. The list is printed in Brandow's *Omitted Chapters from Hotten*.

It can also be seen on the following website:
www.rootsweb.com/~brbwgw/PubForums.htm.

Both of the above lists can also be found in a folder entitled "Some Early Barbadians," held by the BDA (on the open shelves of the search room) and the BML (in the Shilstone Collection). Names are listed on the left with a column for the 1638 list, another for the 1673 list and a fourth column for names included in the Ligon Map (see the "Maps" chapter). Sundry other information for the landholders is recorded in a fifth column.

Returns of hurricane losses 10 October 1780

Landowners made claims for losses incurred in the 1780 hurricane. The return for the parish of St George survives and is held at the BDA under reference RB9/3/9. The document has been restored and is, therefore, fairly easy to use. Names of claimants are given along with numbers of slaves, horses and cattle lost. Valuations are given for losses of furniture, clothes, livestock, buildings and crops.

Slave compensation claims 1836

Following the emancipation of slaves, funds were allocated by the Slave Compensation Commission to compensate the owners. Lists of those compensated can be found at the NLS in the British Parliamentary Papers, Vol. 87. See pp. 245–276 for uncontested claims and pp. 399–401 for litigated claims. Both lists are in date order of the claim, followed by the name of the owner, the number of slaves and the amount claimed. A search of these lists can be time-consuming, as the names are not listed by parish or alphabetically. The list is long, as slave ownership was not restricted to the large landowners; many owned only one slave.

"List of Property Owners of One Acre or More, 1847: Police Magistrates Returns to Governor's Private Secretary"
This can be found on the open shelves of the search room in the BDA. It is organized by parish, then alphabetically by owner, then by name of property and acreage. The parishes of St Andrew and St Philip are missing. There are typed copies of the lists for some parishes. Others are photocopies of the original and the quality of these is variable, some being quite difficult to read.

Published sources with lists

Gandy, Wallace. *The Association Oath Rolls of the British Plantations 1696* (BDA)
In February 1696, following several unsuccessful plots to overthrow William III and reinstate the deposed Stuart monarch, Parliament enacted a statute requiring citizens to sign an Oath of Allegiance to King William. The surviving oath rolls are transcribed in this book and Barbados is included.

The list relating to Barbados can also be seen on the following website: **www.rootsweb.com/~brbwgw/PubForums.htm**.

Handler, J.S., Hughes, R., and E.M. Wiltshire. *Freedmen of Barbados: Names & Notes for Genealogical & Family History Research* (BDA, BML, NLS)
As this chapter shows, there is a shortage of lists for those tracing black ancestry so this small volume is an unusual and important one. The book draws on numerous sources to bring together an alphabetical list of 888 Barbadians with some African ancestry who were either born free or manumitted from enslavement during the slavery period.

**Hughes, Ronald. *The Barbadian Sugar Magnates 1643–1783: Some Jottings,*
JBMHS 35: 211–222 (BDA, BML, NLS)**
This article on the Barbados plantocracy includes the most prominent family and plantation names and describes the intermarriage of some of the families. See Appendix 4 of this guide for the names featured.

Watson, Karl. *The Civilised Island Barbados: A Social History 1750–1816* (BDA, BML, NLS)
This book includes a study of the white population and their land ownership, various offices held and marriages as examples of

intermarriage among the elite families. Dr Watson provides an appendix of "Eighteenth Century Elite Families of Barbados," listing more than 150 names.

Watson, Karl. *Bridgetown Expands in the Late 19th Century: The Creation of the Suburbs of Belleville & Strathclyde,* JBMHS 49: 192–203 (BDA, BML, NLS)
Includes a list of residents and owners.

The Barbados Telephone Directory
It can be interesting to know whether the names you are researching still exist in Barbados. The directory is now available online: **www.barbadosyp.com/whitebook.html.**

Chapter 9

Wills, letters of administration and inventories

Wills

Wills are written by people wishing to set out how their property and money are to be distributed after their death. They can be of enormous interest to family historians as they often name family members and sometimes give an insight into the deceased's relationships with people. The status and wealth of the deceased can be deduced from the property and belongings mentioned. Most people making wills in the past were wealthy but this is not always the case. It is always worth checking for a will, as there is quite a simple procedure to follow.

Contents of wills

Early wills tend to follow the same format, and they can be quite difficult to read. So it is helpful to know what to expect and to be able to home in on the information you are interested in. As an example, we will take the will of Henry Gibbs of Barbados, written in 1731. Firstly we will look at the legal wording and then at an abstract of the relevant details.

In the name of God Amen.
This is the usual opening line of a will.

I Henry Gibbs of the Parish of St Michael in the Island of Barbados Esq.
Place of residence and occupation will often be stated. Women usually gave their occupation as widow or spinster. A married woman could make a will only with her husband's consent and few did.

... being infirm in health but of sound and disposing mind and memory

The majority of wills were written when a person was close to death. It was important that their mental fitness to write the will was stated so that there would be no challenge to it.

... do make and ordain this to be my last will and testament in manner and form following
Real estate is dealt with in a testament and personal belongings and money are bequeathed in a will. This statement therefore brings both together in one document.

I recommend my soul unto the hands of Almighty God and my body to the earth to be decently interred ...
People often gave instructions regarding their burial.

I desire after payment of my debts and funeral charges shall be paid.....
The usual statement made before beginning bequests. This does not mean the person was in debt.

I bequeath to the parish church of ... and the poor of the parish
Sometimes payments such as this are made.

I bequeath my tenements, hereditaments and messuages situate within the parish of...
This covers all buildings owned by the testator along with surrounding land and any outbuildings.

Item
Each bequest starts with this word, followed by the name of the beneficiary and details of the bequest.

I appoint ... my executor
The role of the executors is to have the will proved and to ensure that the wishes of the deceased are carried out. They are usually close family members or friends.

... and I therefore set my hand and seal
The testator's signature will be on the original will. The seal will be that of the lawyer, or the testator if he had a coat of arms.

In the presence of ...
Witnesses to the testator's signature are sometimes people close to the family.

This ...day
The date the will was signed, usually written out in full.

When consulting a will you can save time by copying only an "abstract," containing the key information you really need. Here is an example of an abstract of the will of Henry Gibbs:

Henry Gibbs of the Parish of St Michael in the Island of Barbados, Esq. Dated 25 Dec 1731.
'To my two daughters Helena & Dionesian Gibbs to each of them one shilling and no more on account of their disobedience and undutifulness to me.'
Son Elias Gibbs the sum of £500; £200 to be paid when he reaches the age of 21 and £100 per year for the following three years.
Daughter Hannah Gibbs the sum of £500; £200 to be paid when she reaches the age of 18 and £100 per year for the following three years. The largest necklace of pearl, a pair of Bristol stone buttons set in gold and my jewel and the largest of my two gold bodkins.
Son George Gibbs, £200 and 2 properties in High Street in the Town of St Michael and 2 properties in James Street, St Michael's Town.
Son John Gibbs, plantation in St Michael along with all land, buildings, negroes and slaves.
Mary Cheeseman [no relationship given] 'the messuage or tenement wherein I now dwell with the land thereunto belonging for so long a time as she shall continue to dwell therein and from and after her leaving and ceasing to dwell therein then I give and bequeath the same to my said son George Gibbs and Mary his wife.'
Granddaughter Applia Gibbs daughter of son George Gibbs and Mary his wife, £100.
Executors: Sons George & John Gibbs.
Witnesses: R'd Linden, Arch'd Mitchell, John Eveleigh.
Proved: 6 Jan 1731/2 Barbados.
BDA Ref: RB6/37/163

As this example shows, wills can be useful for piecing together a family. It must be remembered, though, that they will not always give the complete picture and some relationships will be confusing. People mentioned in the will may not be the only living relatives. For instance, daughters were often given a sum on their marriage and so may not appear. Any estranged members of the family could be left out. Although people tended to make their will when it looked as if they hadn't much longer to live, it is still possible that those mentioned in it could have predeceased the testator. Where people were described as sons or daughters they could in fact have been in-laws, whereas sons- and daughters-in-law were possibly stepchildren. Those described as cousins could be any sort of relative or no relation at all.

Where to find wills

1647–1959
Records of wills in Barbados for these years can be found at the BDA. Three series of wills exist: original wills, wills record books and recopied record books.

Very few early original wills are in good enough condition to be seen. Fortunately these were copied into the wills record books many years ago. Due to the deterioration in the state of these books, a further copying was carried out into the "recopied record books." It is these recopied books that are available to the researcher. There are few wills recorded for the early years. As with all copied documents there are errors and omissions. A year of death is helpful when searching for a will and it should be remembered that wills are sometimes proved many years after death.

There are two indexes covering the years 1647–1800 and 1801–1945, and these can be requested in the search room.

Index RB6/44(i)
Wills 1647–1800
This index is organized by surname, then by year. When you find the name you are looking for, you will see two columns of reference numbers. You need those in the second column, which relate to the recopied book volume and page number. The recopied book can be requested using the prefix RB6 followed by the volume number.

Index RB6/44(ii)
Wills 1801–1945
The procedure for this later index is the same as for RB6/44(i) except that only one column of numbers is given. Use this to request the recopied book using the prefix RB4 (not RB6 in this case).

Your request for a recopied book might not be met for a number of reasons:

➢ Although the index is at the BDA, the recopied wills books from 1914 to 1945 are held at the Registration Department. For this period it may be possible to see the original will in the BDA. If the original is unavailable, you could visit the Registration Department to consult the recopied record book. The BDA reference number, name and date should be quoted and there will be a charge. At the time of going to press this was B$20. Alternatively, a copy of the will can be requested; see the next page for details.

BDA: Barbados Department of Archives; BML: Barbados Museum Library

> Recopied books are regularly sent to the Registration Department for copy wills to be made, and so the book requested may be temporarily unavailable at the BDA. If you know the reference number of the book you wish to see in advance of your visit, then a phone call to the BDA to check availability could save you a wasted trip.
> Some of the recopied books are in very poor condition and can no longer be consulted. In this case it may be possible to see the original will if it is still available and in good enough condition.

Original wills to 1959
There are indexes in two volumes 1743–1859 and 1860–1959 for original wills. These can be found on the open shelves of the BDA search room.

Original wills prior to 1914 can only be seen (subject to their condition) if it is not possible to consult the recopied version, as described earlier.

Wills from 1946 have not been copied and so the original can be requested.

Filed wills 1820–1959
An index to wills that were filed and never proved is held on the open shelves of the BDA search room. These can be requested and seen if they are in good condition.

Wills 1960 to date
Wills from 1960 are held at the Registration Department. Staff there will conduct a search; you need to give them a name and date of death.

Obtaining a copy of a will

It is not possible to obtain photocopies, digital scans or other "images" of wills in Barbados. On payment of a fee (per page), staff at the Registration Department will manually extract and type out the contents of a will. This is not to be recommended as there is a risk of errors; the original documents and recopied books are old, handwritten and usually in difficult-to-decipher handwriting. An abstract as described earlier in this chapter, compiled by yourself or a researcher, is usually enough for family history purposes.

If you do, exceptionally, need a typed-out copy these can be obtained from the Registration Department for wills held both there and at the BDA. Overseas researchers should write, fax or telephone, while local researchers must call in person at the office. The reference number, name and date obtained from the BDA should be given for wills up to 1959. From 1960 the name and approximate date of death will be needed. The Registration Department will obtain the relevant record from the BDA (for the earlier wills) and give you a quote for the cost. Payment should then be made, and the copy will be typed and posted.

Finding aids for wills 1639-1725

Sanders, Joanne McRee. *Barbados Records: Wills & Administrations 1639–1725 in 3 Volumes: Vol. 1, 1639–1680, Vol. 2, 1681–1700, Vol. 3, 1701–1725* (BDA, BML, NLS)
This is another remarkable work by Mrs McRee Sanders, along with her volumes on baptisms and marriages in Barbados, and is available on CD-ROM as well as in book form.

Wills are listed in alphabetical order of testators' surnames. Each entry includes all names, dates and places mentioned in the will. There is a name index and everyone mentioned in a will is included in the index, regardless of whether they are beneficiaries, witnesses or the testators themselves. The BDA reference is given for each will, making it an easy matter to request the record book and look at the full will if you wish. This book can also be used as a shortcut for an approximate death date (saving time searching in the burial records) by checking a testator's name against the date his will was proved.

Wills proved in England from 1628–1858

British subjects dying abroad or at sea who owned property in England or Wales had their wills proved in the Prerogative Court of Canterbury (PCC) until 1858. The PCC also had responsibility for wills of West Indians who died in Britain with estate in the West Indies. If you have been unable to find a will, this would be another route to pursue.

Lists of wills relating to Barbados from 1628–1816 and proved in the PCC can be found in V.L. Oliver's *Caribbeana*, Vols. 2 to 4. The name of the testator is given along with the year the will was proved, the name of the register and the reference number.

But there is now a much easier way to consult these wills. They are held at the National Archives (formerly the Public Record Office) in London and are available for searching and downloading online at **www.documentsonline.nationalarchives.gov.uk**.

There is a search facility for wills, and after locating those you are interested in, you will be offered the chance to buy a digital copy, currently for a charge of £3.50 each. Payment can be made by credit card and the document downloaded immediately.

There are several search fields on the site and a name, country and approximate date, among other information, can be entered. For instance, a search on wills for the name Drax between 1628 and 1858 revealed:

Will of John Drax, Gentleman of St Michael, Island of Barbados, West Indies. 16 Jan 1672.

Will of Thomas Drax of St George, Barbados. 22 Dec 1704

Another approach can be fruitful. A search using only the country and date fields for Barbados 1637 to 1700 produced a list of names and dates to scroll through. The following two names were on the list, showing that not all those with wills recorded in England were of the planter class:

John Warner, Grocer of the Island of Barbados. 6 Feb 1671

Robert Lockton, Carpenter of the Island of Barbados. 3 Jul 1671

Wills proved in England from 1858

From 1858 probate became the responsibility of the Principal Probate Registry, now the Principal Registry of the Family Division. These are not available online. To find out how to access them see: **www.nationalarchives.gov.uk/familyhistory/wills/**.

Letters of administration

When someone dies without leaving a will, a relative or friend can apply for authority to settle the estate. They are issued with "letters of administration," and although these provide far less information than a will, they can still be useful to the family historian. The name of the deceased is given, as well as his residence and the date of death. Also included is the name of the person to whom the letters of adminis-tration were granted and his relationship (if any) to the deceased.

Where to find letters of administration

1714–1959
The BDA holds surviving records for these years. There are gaps, particularly in the period 1714 to 1764.

A year of death is needed to request the relevant book. The books are organized by year, and each book has a name index in the front.

1960 to date
Letters of administration from 1960 are held at the Registration Department. Staff there will conduct a search; you will need to give them a name and date of death.

Obtaining a copy of a letter of administration

The procedure for obtaining copies is the same as for wills, described on page 59.

Inventories

In some cases an inventory was filed along with a will or letters of administration. Inventories provide an excellent insight into an ancestor's life and status. They list such items as land, buildings, animals, farming equipment, furniture and household goods. Servants and slaves are often included, sometimes with their names. This can be useful for those researching slave ancestry.

The two examples given here (in summary form) show the range covered by inventories. As with wills they do not always relate to the very wealthy.

Inventory
Thomas Best 31 Oct 1829
Fairy Valley Plantation, Parish of St Thomas.
Land (435 acres) and buildings, value £15,562.10
213 negroes at £55 each, total value £11,715
162 cattle, value £1,762.10
horses, hogs & sheep, value £90
Total value £29,130
There is a separate listing of the 213 slaves by name under the headings men, women, boys, girls.

Inventory
Cuffy Babb, Free Black, Parish of St Lucy 29 Apr 1830
One and a quarter acres of land with a boarded & shingled house £75
A donkey £2.10.0
A mahogany table £1.17.6
Total £79.7.6

Where to find inventories

1764 and 1780–1888
Around 1,800 of these survive for the period 1780–1888 and are held at the BDA. The one remaining earlier inventory relates to William Butler of Christ Church parish in 1764. Many are in good condition, and others have been restored.

An index to inventories can be found on the open shelves of the BDA search room. They are listed by parish and then by surname with separate listings for Bridgetown and Speightstown. "Free black" and "free colored" are listed separately. The year of the inventory is given alongside the surname. This information can then be used to request the document.

Within the index there is a separate listing of plantation names. The year and name of the owner is given. This is particularly useful as wills rarely name the plantation being bequeathed.

Obtaining a copy of an inventory

Copies will be made at the discretion of the BDA staff, depending on the condition of the document.

Finding aids

Handler, J.S., Hughes, R., and E.M. Wiltshire. *Freedmen of Barbados: Names & Notes for Genealogical & Family History Research* (BDA, BML, NLS)
All inventories for free black and free colored people have been analyzed and included in this book. Mr Babb's will (see his inventory described above) is also included, which is fortunate as both the recopied book and the will itself are now in too poor a condition to be consulted. Details of other wills can also be found here for free colored and black people.

Chapter 10

Gravestones and cemetery records

Gravestones and memorials found in cemeteries, churches and churchyards will often give more information than the basic entries in death and burial registers. Their inscriptions (known as monumental inscriptions or MIs) can indicate places and dates of birth, names of parents, children and spouses, occupations and the circumstances of death. Family graves are often grouped together, and you may discover other relatives in this way.

The earliest surviving tombstone in Barbados dates back to 1659 and is now to be found at the Barbados Museum. Formerly at the Christ Church parish church, it is one of only five legible inscriptions to have survived from the church's original site close to the coast at Dover in Christ Church.

Here Lyeth
William Balston
Esq
Dec'd the 26 October
Ano Dom
1659

Such early examples are rare. Many have worn away, cracked and broken or suffered the effects of neglect. Hurricanes have taken their toll, particularly in 1831 when the parish churches of Christ Church, St John, St Joseph, St Lucy, St Peter, St Philip and St Thomas were destroyed and the memorials inside those churches were lost. You may fail to find a monumental inscription for your ancestor for any of these reasons—or perhaps they didn't have one. Gravestones are costly items, and some people were buried with a simple wooden cross or nothing at all to mark the grave.

If you are fortunate enough to find an inscription for one of your ancestors, your research could take quite a leap forward. This long inscription in the churchyard of the parish church of St Thomas gives a wealth of information for the Grannum family:

Fixed on iron railing:

> *The Burial Ground of Richard Grannum*
> *erected by his daughter Amelia G. Grannum.*

On the gravestone:

Sacred to the memory of William Brian Grannum, husband of Sarah Elizabeth Grannum and brother of Sarah Margaret Ellis, Amelia G. Grannum and Mary Grannum. He departed this life, August the 13th 1820 aged 23 years. Also to the memory of Richard Grannum, their father, who died October 6th 1820, aged 52 years. And to their mother Amelia Grant Grannum who died Novr the 22nd 1821, aged 56 years.

This gravestone in St George parish churchyard would be a great help to Susannah Trotman's descendants:

> *Beneath this stone on the*
> *17th anniversary of her marriage*
> *were deposited the earthly remains*
> *of Susannah, the beloved wife of*
> *Joseph Trotman Esqr A.M.*
> *And daughter of*
> *Thos Wm and Frances Bradshaw*
> *Who departed this life in childbirth*
> *On the 22nd of April 1852*
> *Aged 37 years*
> *In sure and certain hope of*
> *The Resurrection to eternal life*
> *Leaving a disconsolate husband*
> *And 9 surviving infant children*
> *To bemoan his loss*

Some inscriptions give us insight into a person's character; who wouldn't want this delightful-sounding lady on their family tree?

> *Kathleen Louise Alone*
> *Wife of*
> *Major John McKenzie Alone*
> *born 25th January 1875*
> *died 9th December 1965*
> *she was pretty to walk with*
> *and witty to talk with*
> *and pleasant to think on*
> *"God rest her soul in peace"*

Locating a gravestone

Before setting off to tour the churchyards and cemeteries of Barbados, there are some sources that will help you narrow your search.

Oliver, Vere Langford. *The Monumental Inscriptions in the Churches & Churchyards of the Island of Barbados* (BDA, BML, NLS)

During a visit to Barbados in 1913/14 Vere Langford Oliver recorded the monumental inscriptions (MIs) in Anglican churches and church-yards on the island, and his work was published in 1915. He provides the full inscriptions, their location in the church or churchyard, and in some cases more biographical details from other sources. A full name index is also included.

www.tombstones.bb

In recent years a group of volunteers has repeated and expanded on the work carried out by Oliver nearly a hundred years ago. All surviving MIs to 1950 in Barbados can be found on this website in index form, and a full transcript of an MI can be obtained by email from the site administrator and creator, Mary Gleadall. There is no charge for this service.

Inscriptions for deaths up to 1950 have been recorded. Where a gravestone records several family members, including some more recent deaths, all are recorded if the earliest death is pre-1950.

The Anglican churches covered by Oliver have been repeated. Some early MIs recorded by him have not survived; these have been included on the website along with a "No" in the "Found" column and page references to his book.

In addition to the Anglican churches, the website covers other denominations such as Roman Catholic, Moravian and Methodist, the burial ground of the Jewish Synagogue and the five municipal cem-eteries that are used by people of the many denominations existing in Barbados. Of these, Westbury alone has more than 3,500 MIs dating from before 1950.

Entries from some burial registers can also be found on the website. Those surviving for the St Ann's Garrison military cemetery covering 1862–1886 are included. These and others are treated in more detail in Chapters 6 and 16.

NLS: National Library Service; JBMHS: Journal of the Barbados Museum & Historical Society

The website can be searched in various ways using the different search fields. A few minutes spent here could save you time combing through burial or death registers. If your search is not successful because an MI no longer exists (or never did), you may have more luck in those records.

Visiting a church or cemetery

Churches

Following a successful search on the website and a follow-up email to the administrator, you have all you need to visit the site where your ancestor is buried. Along with a full transcript of the MI, an indication of its location in the church, churchyard or cemetery will have been supplied. If you are heading for one of the churches, here is an interesting and helpful book worth consulting before your visit:

Hill, Barbara. *Historic Churches of Barbados* (BDA, BML, NLS)

Ms Hill covers Anglican, Roman Catholic, Moravian and Methodist churches, giving their history and a map of their location on the island.

Cemeteries

The Government Sanitation Service Authority manages the five cemeteries in Barbados. The superintendents of three of these cemeteries have offices in the grounds, where the burial registers and plot maps are housed. Copies of the registers are held at the Registration Department and the BDA, as described in earlier chapters. But it is an easy matter to consult the original record during your visit to the cemetery, with the superintendent's permission. However, there are gaps in these original records; dates of those surviving are given here along with contact details.

Westbury Cemetery, Bridgetown
Tel: 430 5033
The earliest burial found and recorded at Westbury took place in 1852. Burial registers held in the cemetery office cover the period 1878 to the present day. Plot records giving the location of headstones are held from 1934 to the present day.

St James Cemetery and St Peter Cemetery

Tel: 419 7505

Administration of these two is combined at the office located in St James Cemetery, Cemetery Road, St James. The earliest recorded burials took place in 1826 in St Peter and 1888 in St James.

Surviving burial registers for St James cover:
- 2 Jan 1913–10 Aug 1923
- 21 Sep 1940–19 Feb 1952
- 29 Dec 1959 to the present day

Surviving burial registers for St Peter cover:
- 25 May 1961 to the present day

Christ Church Cemetery and Bushey Park Cemetery

Tel: 418 6500

Administration of these two is combined at the Christ Church Cemetery located next to the Christ Church parish churchyard.

Bushey Park is a recently established cemetery, and no burials took place there before 1950. The earliest recorded burial in the Christ Church Cemetery was in 1923.

Records before 1969 were destroyed by fire.

Coral Ridge Cemetery and Crematorium

Coral Ridge opened in 2003 and is the location of the first cremation in Barbados. Burials and cremations here are too recent for our purposes.

Chapter 11

Newspapers and directories

Newspapers

Newspapers are a source of many different types of information. Apart from notices of birth, marriage and death they also name individuals involved in legislative proceedings, accidents and other newsworthy events. Ships arriving and leaving are recorded and prominent citizens on board named. Advertisements for runaway slaves include detailed physical descriptions and the amount of reward offered for the slave's capture. Business advertisements for shops, trades and hotels identify individuals involved in various trades and commercial activities.

Newspapers can be used to locate information on an individual, or they can be browsed to see what events were taking place when your ancestors were alive. In 1854 the newspapers were full of news of the cholera epidemic sweeping through the island. The Barbadian newspaper of 5 July reports deaths of 9,000 with an estimate of 5,300 for St Michael alone. We now know that the final total exceeded 20,000. A longer than usual death announcements column was published on 26 July 1854, although only a fraction of those who died are recorded.

Details of some of those listed are reproduced below. The list makes interesting reading, showing how the cholera, while spreading along one street in Bridgetown (The Roebuck, now known as Roebuck Street) was also affecting those at the other end of the island in St Lucy. Rather poignantly the same newspaper published "preventatives" for cholera, this being a time when the causes of the disease were not understood.

The Barbadian 26 July 1854
Died:
Recently in the Roebuck, Mrs Hazlewood, three daughters and one son.
On the 23rd, in the Roebuck, Samuel son of Mr John Welsh.

Same day in the Roebuck, Mr John Taylor
Same day, in the same street, Mrs Roach
On Saturday the 24th inst. At Brighton, the residence of J.F. Best Esq., George H. Gordon, eldest son of Robert Gordon Esq., Merchant of Dominica, after a short illness of eleven hours of Cholera. Also on the same day in the City, of the same disease, Augustus, third brother of the above named J.F. Best. Both bodies were interred on Sunday after morning service, in the Burial Ground of St Mary's Chapel.
On the 24th, at "Wakenham," parish of St Lucy, Mary Jane, wife of Shadrack Kellman, Esq. And on the afternoon of the same day, Ann Cragg, his daughter. Both these ladies fell victim to Cholera, the former after 17 hours, and the latter after 8 hours illness.
On Saturday night last, of the prevailing Epidemic at the residence of her father, Mary Sims, second daughter of Edward Weeks Esq., of "Roses," St Philip's parish.

Announcements of birth, marriage and death can save time looking through registers. The following announcements tell us that Matthew and Charlotte Cromartie had four children prior to Charlotte's death in 1839. We could now search for their baptism details, or earlier newspapers may record their birth.

The Barbadian 17 August 1824
Married: Yesterday morning by Rev RF King Matthew Cromartie Esq to Miss Charlotte Lloyd eldest daughter of the late William Draper Lloyd Esq.

The Barbadian 31 July 1839
Died: On 29 inst. At White River Estate, Charlotte wife of Matthew Cromartie Esq, 3 days after her confinement with her fourth child. Buried at the Cathedral.

A marriage that took place elsewhere will not appear in the records for Barbados. This newspaper announcement could solve the mystery, if the records did not include a marriage for Joseph Rogers.

The Times, Barbados 22 December 1865
Married: on Nov 28, in Camp-Street, Demerara [Guyana] Joseph Beard Welch Rogers, of Barbados, to Sarah Elizabeth, only daughter of the late Thomas P Hart, formerly proprietor of the plantation Haag's Bosche in Demerara.

When searching for an ancestor's death or burial record, you would not usually expect to find they lived more than 100 years. This notice in 1829 would save a lot of searching. It also gives an idea of the size of the final family tree!

The Barbadian 13 March 1829
Died in this Town on Wednesday last, at the advanced age of 105 years, Mrs Ann Ashby, an old inhabitant of the coloured community, leaving five children, 25 grandchildren, 60 great-grandchildren, and 20 great-great-grandchildren.

Other items in the newspapers add to our knowledge of individuals, as these two extracts show:

The Barbadian 16 January 1829
Mr Nathaniel Fitzpatrick will open school at the Farm, St Philip, on 2 Feb. Reading, writing, arithmetic, English Grammar, Geography and History for £15 per annum; competent teachers will attend weekly to teach Music and Dancing.

The Times, Barbados 2 March 1866
Congratulations: The Editor congratulates Mr R. Gooding, Police Magistrate of St Thomas, on the achievement of his son Dr J.H. Gooding, in practice in Cheltenham, where the London Medical Times of Jan. 1866 reports his successful performance of a rare and dangerous operation – Ovariotomy.

This is typical of a runaway slave notice:

Runaway from the subscriber in July last; a
Negro WOMAN by the name of Jenny, about 5 feet
4 or 5 inches high, a very black skin, slender made,
she has a little impediment in her speech, and the fin-
gers on one hand appear drawn. She has a husband
by the name of Tom Pigeon, a short, yellow man,
formerly belonging to the Widow Barrow, deceased,
at present the property of Mr. Jacob Belgrave who
it is supposed has her concealed at some of his con-
nections. – A reward of Ten Guineas will be given for
apprehending and delivering the said Woman to the
subscriber; and an additional reward of Five Guineas
for such information as will lead to conviction any
white or free coloured person harbouring the said slave
- Masters of vessels are cautioned against taking her
from the Island, as the law will be enforced against
such offenders.

Bay; Sept 26 – 3a   **S.F. COLLYMORE**

Barbados Mercury & Bridgetown Gazette, 3 Oct 1815

Locating old newspapers

There are a number of ways to approach this. The most comprehensive collection of newspapers in Barbados is that held by the NLS. The newspapers are viewed on microfilm, and there is no personal name index. A full listing of their holdings is given in this chapter, but first we will look at alternative approaches.

Old Barbados Newspapers (BML)

This is a collection of early newspapers, reproduced and published in two large volumes by Jim Lynch, covering:
Volume I
Barbados Globe & Colonial Advocate
4 September 1837, 8 and 15 February 1838, and the period from 28 March 1839 to 9 April 1840
Volume II
Barbados Mercury & Bridgetown Gazette
8 October 1815, and the period from 15 January 1839 to 28 January 1840

Oliver, Vere Langford. *Caribbeana*, 6 vols. (BDA, BML, NLS)

For more details about this publication, see Chapter 5. Among the wide collection of genealogical data in *Caribbeana* are extracts of birth, marriage and death announcements in newspapers. They can be found in Vols. 2 and 3, and there is a name index. Coverage is as follows:

Barbados Mercury & Bridgetown Gazette: 1805–1818 births, marriages and deaths.

Barbados Chronicle & Caribbean Courier: December 1807–November 1809, births, marriages and deaths.

Barbados Mercury: 1783–1784, marriages and deaths.

Journal of the Barbados Museum & Historical Society (BDA, BML, NLS)

Over many years the *Journal* published extracts from old newspapers, including announcements of birth, marriage and death and other items with residents' names mentioned. There is a personal name index to the *Journal*, of enormous value when using these records. For details see Chapter 5. The coverage of newspaper extracts is given on the following page, along with the *Journal* volume where they can be found.

JBMHS	Newspaper	Period covered
Vol. 1	*The Barbadian*	Dec 1822 – Dec 1825
Vol. 2	*The Barbadian*	Dec 1825 – Dec 1828
Vol. 3	*The Barbadian*	Jan 1829 – Dec 1830 Jan – Nov 1831 missing Dec 1831 – Dec 1832
Vol. 4	*The Barbadian*	Dec 1832 – May 1835
Vol. 5	*The Barbadian*	May 1835 – Mar 1836
Vol. 6	*The Barbadian*	Mar 1836 – Jul 1837
Vol. 7	*The Barbadian*	Jul 1837 – Sep 1838
Vol. 8	*The Barbadian*	Sep 1838 – Feb 1840
Vol. 9	*The Barbadian*	Feb 1840 – Jun 1841
Vol. 10	*The Barbadian*	Jun 1841 – Dec 1842
Vol. 11	*The Barbadian*	Jan 1843 – Jul 1844
Vol. 12	*The Barbadian*	Jul 1844 – Dec 1844 1845 missing Jan 1846 – Nov 1846
Vol. 13	*The Barbadian*	Dec 1846 – Aug 1847
Vol. 14	*The Barbadian*	Aug 1847 – Jul 1848
Vol. 15	*The Barbadian*	Jul 1848 – Dec 1849
Vol. 16	*Barbados Mercury*	Apr 1783 – Dec 1784
Vol. 17	*Barbados Mercury*	Jul 1787 – Mar 1789
Vol. 18	*Barbados Mercury*	Jun 1819 – Dec 1819
Vol. 19	*Barbados Globe Official Gazette & Colonial Advocate*	Jan 1850 – Jun 1850
Vol. 20	*Barbados Globe Official Gazette & Colonial Advocate*	Jul 1850 – Dec 1850 Jan 1852 – Jul 1852
Vol. 21	*Barbados Globe Official Gazette & Colonial Advocate*	Jul 1852 – Dec 1853
Vol. 22	*The Barbadian*	Jan 1854 – Jun 1855
Vol. 23	*The Barbadian*	Jul 1855 – Feb 1856
Vol. 24	*The Barbadian*	Feb 1856 – May 1857
Vol. 25	*The Barbadian*	May 1857 – Dec 1858
Vol. 26	*The Liberal*	Jul 1858 – Jul 1859
Vol. 27	*The Barbadian*	Jan 1860 – Sep 1860
Vol. 28	*The Barbadian*	Oct 1860 – Sep 1861
Vol. 29	*The Barbadian,* *Barbados Globe Official Gazette & Colonial Advocate*	Oct 1861 – Mar 1862 Jan 1862 – Jun 1862
Vol. 30	*The Times* *Barbados Globe Official Gazette & Colonial Advocate*	Jan 1863 –Dec 1863 (1864 missing) Jan 1865 – Mar 1865 Jul 1862 – Dec 1862
Vol. 31	*The Times*	Apr 1865 – Jun 1866
Vol. 32	*The Times*	Jul 1866 – Dec 1868
Vol. 33	*The Times*	Jan 1869 Feb 1870 – Dec 1870

Original newspapers on microfilm at the National Library Service

See Chapter 3, "List of archives," for guidance on accessing these microfilms.

Newspaper	Dates available (with some gaps)
Barbados Mercury	Apr 5 1783 – Dec 11 1784
	Jul 21 1787 – Apr 11 1789
Barbados Gazette & Intelligence	Jun 30 1787 – Feb 14 1789
Barbados Mercury & Bridgetown Gazette	Jan 8 1805 – Dec 30 1806
	Jan 3 1807 – Jan 1825
The Barbadian	Dec 14 1822 –1849
	1854 –1858, 1860 – 61
Barbados Globe & Colonial Advocate	Sep 4 1837 – May 19 1926
The Liberal	Feb 13 1839 – April 8 1840
	Mar 25 & Jun 9 1864
West Indian	Mar 7 1839 – May 29 1874
	Dec 11 1874, 1876 – 1884, Jan–Jun 1885
The Sun	Feb 19 – Apr 4 1840
The Times	1863, 1865 – Feb 1 1871
	Feb 10 1872 – Feb 1 1873
	Feb 10 1875 – Dec 1876, 1877
	1884 – Sep 4 1895
Barbados People	Mar 23 – Aug 22 1876
Penny Paper	Jun – Dec 1876
The Sentinel	Sep – Dec 1876
Two Penny Paper	Jun – Sep 1877
Weekly Recorder	Nov 20 1897 – Dec 30 1897
	1900 – 1909, Jan 10 – Aug 13 1910
	Oct 3 – Dec 31 1951
	Jan 1952 – Apr 1953
	Jan 1958 – Dec 1959
Barbados Daily News	Jan 1900 – Jun 30 1922
	Jun 1960 – Dec 1964
	1965 – 1967
Barbados Standard	Apr 29 1911 – Dec 28 1912
Barbados Standard weekend edition	1913 – 1921
Barbados Advocate	Jun 27 1916 – May 1963
	1964 – Aug 2002
Barbados Herald	Feb 1 1919 – Dec 1929
	Jan – May 23 1930
	Apr 4 1931 – Dec 1943
	Jan 8 – Nov 25 1944
	May 19 – Dec 29 1945
Weekly Illustrated	May 10 – Dec 27 1919
	May 1 1920 – Aug 13 1921
	Dec 24 & 31 1921
Barbados Times	Jan 10 1920 – Aug 17 1921
Barbados Observer	Nov 10 1934 – Jun 7 1975
Barbados Recorder	Oct 3 1951 – Apr 1953,1958, 1959
Daily Gleaner	May 1956 – Dec 1990
Beacon	1958 – 1967

The present-day newspapers in Barbados are *The Nation* and *The Barbados Advocate*:

www.nationnews.com
www.barbadosadvocate.com

Directories and almanacs

Other publications of interest to family historians are directories, almanacs, magazines and other publications listing people. Taking the contents of the *Barbados Yearbook & Who's Who 1933/34* as an example, we can see the value of consulting these.

The *Yearbook* includes numerous lists of people such as doctors, veterinary surgeons, dentists, druggists, barristers, solicitors, JPs, rectors and vicars. There is a business directory with names listed under such headings as grocery and provision dealers, importers and exporters, jewelers and stationers. There is a list of estates with acreage and name of proprietors. Members of the House of Assembly are named, as are those serving on the General Hospital Board and as trustees of the Public Library and as members of the vestries, among many other bodies. Governors of Barbados 1625–1933 and Colonial Secretaries 1863–1931 are also listed. Two hundred biographies of prominent citizens are given, some with photographs, the following being a typical example:

Hoad, Edward Lisle Goldsworthy. Factory Manager. Born 1896, Barbados. Ed. Combermere School & Harrison College. Manager Vaucluse Sugar Factory. Recreation: Cricket. Rep. Barbados in inter-col. tournaments since 1922. Rep. W.I. on tour in England 1928 & 1933. Address: Vaucluse, St Thomas.

Another publication worth consulting is *The Bajan* magazine, published from September 1953 to December 1992, initially with twelve issues per year, reducing to six in later years. The magazine features a "People" section where marriages, wedding anniversaries, obituaries, business appointments and other events are recorded, frequently with photographs. More in-depth studies of people are to be found in articles entitled "Interesting People." For example, in the issue of Nov/Dec 1986 *65 Years for Goddard Enterprises Ltd* describes the life of Joe Goddard, born 1874 in Clifton Hall, St John, and his rise to be one of the most successful merchants in Bridgetown. A photograph shows Joe with his daughter and nine sons. Other issues feature obituaries of several Goddard family members. The April 1979 issue has an article by Warren Alleyne entitled *From Slave to Businessman* about the life of London Bourne (1793–1869) and his rise from slavery to become one of Bridgetown's most prominent merchants.

The BDA & BML have card indexes for *The Bajan* with both subject and personal names listed.

A full listing of the whereabouts of these and other publications is given below.

Barbados Department of Archives

Directories and other periodical publications	Years available
The Barbados Almanac	1860, 1870
Barbados Business & General Directory	1887
Barbados Diamond Jubilee Directory & General West Indian Advertiser	1898
Handbook of Barbados	1907
The Barbados Handbook	1912, 1913, 1914
Leverick's Directory of Barbados	1921
The Barbados Yearbook	1933/4 – 1937
The Barbados Business Directory & Tourist Guide	1934
Social Directory of Barbados	1938
Advocate Year Book & Who's Who	1951
The Bajan	Sep 1953 – Dec 1992

Barbados Museum Library

Directories and other periodical publications	Years available
The Barbados Almanac	1816, 1829, 1832, 1838, 1848, 1850, 1854, 1861, 1863, 1865, 1871, 1882, 1890, 1892, 1898
Barbados Business & General Directory	1887, 1898, 1899, 1902, 1905/6, 1907/8
The Barbados Handbook	1912, 1913, 1914
Colonial Office List	1913, 1939
Barbados Civil List	Various years from the 1920s to 1976
Leverick's Directory of Barbados	1921
Barbados Yearbook & Who's Who	1934, 1935, 1937, 1964
Social Directory of Barbados	1938
Barbados Annual Review	1945 – 1953
Advocate Year Book & Who's Who	1951
The Bajan	Sep 1953 – Dec 1992

BDA: Barbados Department of Archives; BML: Barbados Museum Library

National Library Service

Directories and other periodical publications	Years available
The West Indies Illustrated	1909
The Barbados Handbook	1913, 1914
The Barbados Yearbook & Who's Who	1933/4, 1935,1937, 1964
The Bajan	Sep 1953 – Dec 1992
Barbados Annual Review	Dec 1954 – Nov 1955

Chapter 12

Deeds and powers of attorney

In Barbados, records grouped together under the heading of Deeds include land conveyances, leases, marriage settlements, bills of lading, letters of exchange and court decisions. Those relating to the owner-ship of land are of particular interest to the family historian as they tell us where and when people lived and what they did with their land. A deed could, for instance, simply transfer ownership from one person to another, or it could provide for a lease of property from a landlord to a tenant for a specified period. Members of wealthy families often entered into marriage settlements where a father transferred land or other property to his son or his daughter and her husband-to-be. These are particularly helpful, as they provide information about the family's property as well as family names and relationships, and in some cases they are the only surviving record of a marriage. Manumissions (grants of freedom from slavery) are also found in this group of records; these are looked at separately in the "Slave records" chapter.

A power of attorney is a particular type of deed by which the person giving it (the grantor) authorizes someone else (the grantee) to act as his legal representative. Powers of attorney are not normally a partic-ularly fruitful source of information for family history. In a small island community like Barbados, however, where property owners and other business people were often away for years at a time, they were widely used. They provide useful details such as plantation names, overseas addresses, occupations and sometimes relationships.

Deeds

Deeds for the period 1636 to 1949 are held at the BDA. There are original deeds books covering the years 1647 to 1949 (reference: RB1) and recopied records for the period 1636 to 1833 (reference: RB3). We will look at each of these separately.

Original deeds 1647–1800

This is not an easy set of records to access. Only about half the deeds from 1647–1718 survive and the period 1718–1781 is incomplete.

There is no separate index to deeds prior to 1800. Some volumes for this period have indexes within them but many have none.

The main problem with the earlier deeds is that they are in poor condition and frequently cannot be seen. It is worth requesting a book for the period you are interested in, while accepting that the staff member may not be able to meet your request. An alternative is then to look for a recopied deed. These are described on the next page.

Original deeds 1801–1949

These later years are easier to access. The index of grantors (labeled "Deeds") starts from 1801. The index for grantees (labeled "Counter Deeds") starts from 1879.

Indexes RB2/1–11 cover 1801–1907. For 1908–1949 the year required should be requested.

The indexes are organized by year, then by initial letter of the surname. The type of record is given along with a volume and page number. To request the original deed book, the volume number should be given with the prefix RB1.

Depending on its condition, the original book may be brought to you. Microfilm copies are available for the years 1834–1882 (RB1/288–364). From 1883–1949 the books are generally in good condition. If you are not able to see a book for 1801–1833, you could try accessing the recopied records (see next page).

In this example, a search in index RB2/7 for Clarke revealed a deed of gift.

Deed No.	Grantee		Grantor	Type	Volume No.	Page No.
614	Clarke J.A.	from	Rogers A.M.	Deed of gift	368	370

The original deed book was requested under reference RB1/368.

Deed of gift dated 6 March 1879
Anna Maria Rogers, spinster of the parish of Christ Church

to Jemima Ann Clarke, spinster of the parish of Christ Church
2 roods of land in Christ Church butting and bounding on lands of
Mr George Henry Clarke, Anna Maria Rogers, John Rogers, Philip
Rogers and the public road.
Witnesses: Samuel Taylor, George H. Clarke, William H. Alleyne
BDA Ref: RB1/368/370

This is typical of the way land is described in these records. The size of
the plot and its position in relation to land belonging to others are
given. The Clarke and Rogers families owned several pieces of land in
Christ Church, as we discover here, and the family names may prove
helpful for family research. The deed does not help us identify the
location of the land within the parish, however.

Recopied Deeds 1636–1833

The recopied deeds books are held in series RB3 at the BDA and cover
the years 1636–1833. Only about a quarter of the original deeds were
copied, so this is by no means a complete listing.

The deeds are indexed separately for grantor and grantee (counter
deeds) under the following references (note some overlapping of
dates).
- RB3/48 1636–1730
- RB3/49 1635–1730 Counter
- RB3/50 1680–1833
- RB3/51 1680–1833 Counter

The indexes are organized by year, then by initial letter of the
surname. Unlike the indexes for original deeds, the type of transaction
is not given. Two numbers are provided, for the recopied record book
volume and page.

To request the relevant book, use the prefix RB3 followed by the
volume number.

There are some problems to look out for when using these indexes:

> The indexes are divided alphabetically in the same format as an
  address book. For some letters the allocated pages are full, and the
  names then continue under another letter. For instance RB3/49 has
  F in the H section and H in the P section.
> Years are roughly in chronological order; look out for years
  appearing out of order.
> As mentioned above, only about a quarter of the original deeds
  were recopied.

> The deeds were copied haphazardly, and the volumes are not in any chronological order.
> As with all copied documents there will be errors in the copying.
> Some deeds were recorded in the grantor indexes but not in the grantee indexes. For example, this search in the indexes was successful for the names of both parties:
Counter deed index RB3/49
1687 CUFFLY Thomas from RICE Walter Vol. 25/ Page 147
Deed index RB3/50
1687 RICE Walter to CUFFLY Thomas Vol. 25/ Page 147

Whereas this one had been indexed only once:
Counter deed index RB3/49
1681 HOTHERSAL Thomas from LITTLETON Edward Vol. 14/ Page 314
Deeds index RB3/50 no entry

> Some deeds (and powers of attorney) involve more than one grantor or grantee. In these cases a name and "et al" is given in the index. Your search for a name can sometimes be frustrated if the person you hope to find is not the principal name.

Deeds from 1950

These are held at the Land Registry, Chelsea House, Chelsea Road, St Michael:
Tel: (246) 429 9513.

A personal search can be made for a charge, currently B$5 per book covering one year. Alternatively a member of staff will make a search for you, though they do not carry out extensive research. The names of the parties and approximate year should be given.

Powers of Attorney

Powers of Attorney 1698–1947

Records for this period are held at the BDA under reference RB7/29–119. There are four indexes:
- RB8/1 1698–1864
- RB8/2 1867–1885
- RB8/3 1886–1919
- RB8/4 1920–1947

The indexes are organized alphabetically by the surname of the grantor and then by year. Indexes after 1886 list the entry twice, under the grantor and grantee. When using these indexes, be aware that some letters overflow into other letters, for instance in RB8/4 J is listed in L, and Y in Q.

A search in the index RB8/1 for John Horsham revealed this entry in 1782:

Grantor		Grantee	Volume	Page
Horsham John	To	Thomas Pollard et al	43	147

To request the record book, the prefix RB7 was used followed by volume number 43. The entry on page 147 gives us this information:

John Horsham of the parish of St Michael, Practitioner in Physick and Surgery but shortly intending to parts beyond the seas...appoint Thomas Pollard of the parish of St Michael, Physician and William Horsham of the parish of St Michael, Goldsmith and Jeweller, to be my true and lawful attorneys. Witnesses: Richard Wilson, Wm Thos Phillips, Jno Sutton Taylor
24 May 1782
BDA Ref: RB7/43/147

The following power of attorney provides some interesting information for a group of spinsters (possibly sisters) and was found by consulting the index RB8/1:

Grantor		Grantee	Volume	Page
Gibbons Fanny et al	To	Sir J.G. Alleyne	43	204

Fanny Gibbons, Eliza. Hannah Gibbons, Martha Gibbons of Dalchet in the County of Bucks, Spinsters, appoint Sir John Gay Alleyne of Barbados and Scarvon (sic) Henrick Gibbons of Barbados to be their lawful attorneys. Authorisation is given for the attorneys to take possession and manage the plantation named Mullins in the parish of St Peter.
21 Apr 1783
BDA Ref: RB7/43/204

Powers of Attorney 1661–1849

An additional collection of powers of attorney, (reference: RB7/1–21) covering 1661–1849 is held at the BDA. These are not included in the indexes described above, making them difficult to use, though some have their own index. Most are in poor condition and cannot be seen. For a full list, including their condition, see Class List I (red ring binder) on the BDA search room shelves.

Powers of Attorney from 1948

These are held at the Land Registry, Chelsea House, Chelsea Road, St Michael:
Tel: (246) 429 9513.
A personal search can be made for a charge, currently B$5 per book covering one year. Alternatively a member of staff will make a search for you, though they do not carry out extensive research. The names of the parties and approximate year should be given.

Obtaining copies of deeds and powers of attorney

It is not possible to obtain photocopies, digital scans or other "images'"of deeds and powers in Barbados. On payment of a fee (per page), staff at the Land Registry will manually extract and type out the contents. This is not to be recommended as there is a risk of errors; the records are old, handwritten and usually in difficult to decipher handwriting. The relevant information recorded by yourself or a researcher is usually sufficient for family history purposes.

If you do, exceptionally, need a typed-out copy, these can be obtained from The Land Registry, Chelsea House, Chelsea Road, St Michael, Tel: (246) 429 9513. There is no email address at present. For documents held at the BDA, quote their reference and the names of the parties. A charge per page is payable in cash.

Chapter 13

Plantation and land ownership

One of the most commonly asked questions by people researching their family history in Barbados is "Where will I find plantation records?" Some are looking for a plantation-owning ancestor and others for a plantation slave. Plantation records are private records, so they tend to be in private hands and few are available to researchers. Even those that are available to us are of limited use for family history purposes as they mainly deal with the day-to-day administration of the plantation and most are 20th-century records. There are a few exceptions and these are listed in this chapter.

The search for plantation owners has been made easier by the work of Ronald Hughes and Cecil Queree, and there are published sources that can be helpful.

For those interested in slaves, another approach to try is the slave registers compiled in the period 1817–1834. See the "Slave records" chapter for a full description of these records.

Plantation records

Messrs Bovell & Skeete, accountants of Bridgetown, deposited a large collection of plantation records at the BDA, but as they are mainly accounts books they are of limited interest for family history research. A full listing can be found in:
Chandler, M.J. *A Guide to Records in Barbados* (BDA, BML, NLS)

The BDA holds the original records for Drax Hall Plantation. They also have copies of records for Turners Hall Plantation dating back to the 18th century, the originals being in the Fitzherbert collection in England.

The BML holds a collection of original plantation records, which can be seen with prior permission of a curator of the Museum. Access will be granted depending on their condition.

The plantations concerned are as follows:
Avon, Bissex Hill, Bourbon, Carlton, Claybury, Colleton, Cottage Grove, Forster Hall, Frizer, Haynesfield, Holder, Hopewell, Kingsland, Newcastle, Newton, Rock Dundo, Searles, Sion Hill, Sunbury, Walkes Spring and Westmoreland.

Barbados Plantations: Index to plantation owners 1630–1846

Over many years the historian Ronald Hughes has compiled data on plantation ownership in Barbados using deeds, wills, maps, census records, newspapers, surveyors' plans and correspondence. Mr Hughes has granted permission for his collection of more than 2,000 surnames to be published on the website **www.plantations.bb**.

You can search by surname or plantation name. These were the results of searches for the Burnt House Plantation and the Dottin family:

Plantation	Parish	Year	Owner
Burnt House	St Andrew	1704	Dottin, William
Burnt House	St Andrew	1745	Dottin, James (President)*
Burnt House	St Andrew	1776	Maycock, Dottin
Burnt House	St Andrew	1777	Blackett, Stephen
Burnt House	St Andrew	1825	Jordan, Joseph W.
Burnt House	St Andrew	1846	Clarke, Sir Robert Bowcher, C.J.

Plantation	Parish	Year	Owner
Baxter's	St Andrew	1704	Dottin, William
Baxter's	St Andrew	1704	Dottin, John
Burnt House	St Andrew	1704	Dottin, William
Greenland	St Andrew	1704	Dottin, William
Haggatt's	St Andrew	1704	Dottin, William
Lascelles	St James	1721	Dottin, Joseph
Baxter's	St Andrew	1725	Dottin, Ann
Nicholas	St Andrew, St Peter	1727	Dottin, Joseph
Mount Edge	St Thomas	1734	Dottin, Thomas
Husbands	St James	1735	Dottin, Joseph
Nicholas	St Andrew, St Peter	1735	Dottin, Joseph
Baxter's	St Andrew	1745	Dottin, James (President)*
Burnt House	St Andrew	1745	Dottin, James (President)*
Haggatt's	St Andrew	1745	Dottin, James (President)*
Mount Edge	St Thomas	1759	Dottin, John

BDA: Barbados Department of Archives; BML: Barbados Museum Library

Plantation	Parish	Year	Owner
Farley Hill	St Peter	1760	Dottin, Abel
Greenland	St Andrew	1760	Dottin, Abel
Baxter's	St Andrew	1783	Dottin, John (President)*
Farley Hill	St Peter	1783	Dottin, Samuel Rous
Greenland	St Andrew	1784	Dottin, Abel Rous
Clifton Hall	St John	1806	Dottin, Elizabeth
Clifton Hall	St John	1809	Dottin, Abel Rous
Coverley	Christ Church	1825	Dottin, Abel Rous
Coverley	Christ Church	1846	Dottin, Abel Rous

*President was the most senior position in the Barbados Council. In the Governor's absence, the President took over the administration of the Government. See the "Island administration" chapter for more information.

Hughes and Queree plantation ownership records 1630s to the 1950s

These cover the same data as described above with the addition of another hundred years and were compiled by Mr Hughes and added to by Mr Queree. They can be found at the BDA, handwritten and collected together in ring binders. They are organized alphabetically by plantation name and separately by owners' names. It is hoped that these records will be added to **www.plantations.bb** in due course.

Other records of landowners

The BML holds a card index (again the work of Mr Queree). Entries are filed separately under "Estates" and "Estate owners" and cover the 1840s to the 20th century.

The directories and almanacs described in Chapter 12 frequently list estates and their owners.

The BDA holds a *Schedule of Land and their Respective Owners in Barbados 1919* in two volumes on the open shelves of the BDA search room. This is a listing of landowners with plots from large to very small; acreage is given and it is organized by parish. It would help to know the parish of residence of the person you are tracing. Some areas are omitted altogether, for example "Holetown – the town proper." Omissions are listed in the front.

This chapter's "Further reading" is worth checking for the names you are interested in. All the works listed have indexes that include personal names. For instance, Addinton Forde's book names numerous individuals with plantations, streets and areas named after them.

NLS: National Library Service; JBMHS: Journal of the Barbados Museum & Historical Society

Warren Alleyne gives us the origin of street names in Bridgetown, for example, on page 110:

GILL'S ROAD – The construction of this road, which leads from Whitepark Road to Roebuck Street, was started in April 1880. Its name derives from Mr W.H. Gill who had recently established a foundry at the Whitepark end of the road.

HIGGINSON'S LANE – Named after John Higginson, merchant (died at Liverpool, England, 1834). John Higginson once owned the property now called Bishop's Court.

Further reading

Addinton Forde, G. *Place-Names of Barbados* (BML, NLS)

Alleyne, Warren. *Historic Bridgetown* (BDA, BML, NLS)

Fraser, H.S., Hughes, R. *Historic Houses of Barbados* (BDA, BML, NLS)

Greenidge, Morris. *Holetown Barbados: Settlement Revisited* (BDA, BML, NLS)

Chapter 14

Maps

For research into landowning families in Barbados, maps are an invaluable source of information. All the old maps described in this chapter include names of landowners, the first map dating from just a few years after the island was settled by the English. Some family names appear repeatedly. For instance Charles, George and Robert Terrill were included in the "List of inhabitants who possessed more than 10 acres of land in the year 1638" (described in Chapter 8), and the Terrill name is mentioned on maps spanning nearly 200 years.

The old maps described below can all be seen in the galleries of the Barbados Museum. For a more detailed study of them, copies may be viewed in the BML by prior arrangement with a Museum curator. The BDA also holds copies, which can be requested in the search room.

Reproductions of the Ligon, Ford, Bowen and Mayo maps can be purchased in the Barbados Museum shop.

The major old maps

Ligon's map, about 1650
Richard Ligon's *True and Exact History of the Island of Barbados*, published in London in 1657, contains the earliest known map of Barbados. Between 200 and 250 plantation owners' names are listed, some more than once. Further evidence for the period suggests that this list is incomplete.

The list can be found in a folder entitled *Some Early Barbadians*, held by the BDA (on the open shelves of the search room) and the BML (in the Shilstone collection).

Ford's map, about 1680
Compiled by Richard Ford, a surveyor living in Bridgetown, this is the first systematic map of the island, and it identifies more than 800 plantations by name of owner.

Moll's map 1728
Described as *A New Map of the Island of Barbadoes containing all the Parishes and Principal Plantations; together with ye Forts, Lines, Batteries, Roads &c. By H. Moll Geographer.*

A reproduction, with the names of property owners clearly legible, can be seen in D.L. Kent's *Barbados & America* (BDA, BML, NLS).

Bowen's map 1747
See Figure 5 on pages 94-95

Mayo's map 1756
A New & Accurate map of the Island of Barbadoes Divided into its Parishes: Containing all the Towns, Plantations, Forts, Capes, Bays etc.

This is a later, improved edition of Mayo's map of 1722, which was the first to show parish boundaries. It includes a plan of Bridgetown and many property owners' names.

An early copy of the Mayo map had a list of subscribers attached, many of them residents of Barbados. The list, along with a foldout Mayo map, can be seen in *George Washington's Visit to Barbados 1751* (BDA, BML), compiled by Richard B. Goddard.

Barrallier's map 1825
This map has a very useful list, printed in its lower corners, of approximately 400 plantations and "places" with their owners' names and parish locations.

Present-day maps

A recent map of the island is a great help to the family historian, and the following are available from the Lands & Survey Department, Mahogany Court, Wildey, St Michael, Barbados, Tel: (246) 426 3959.

Ordnance Survey Map of Barbados
Scale 1:50,000.

Barbados divided into twelve sub-sections
Twelve maps, each to a scale of 1:10,000

Bridgetown street map
Scale 1:5,000

BDA: Barbados Department of Archives; BML: Barbados Museum Library

Further reading

Campbell, P.F. *Ligon's Map*, JBMHS 34: 108–112 (BDA, BML, NLS)

Campbell, Tony. *The Printed Maps of Barbados* (BDA, BML, NLS)

Shilstone, E.M. *Descriptive Lists of Maps of Barbados,* JBMHS 5: 57–84 (BDA, BML, NLS)

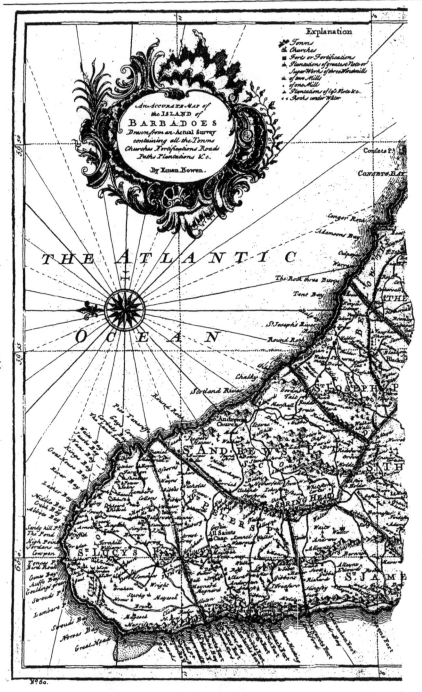

Figure 5   Bowen's map of Barbados, 1747

BDA: Barbados Department of Archives; BML: Barbados Museum Library

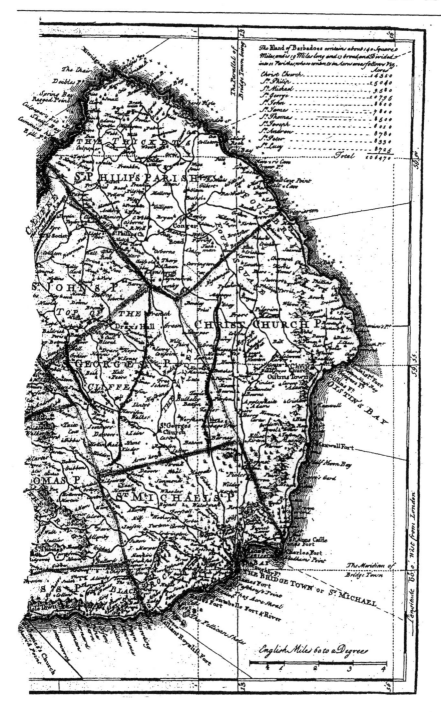

Chapter 15

Island administration

As early as 1629 the Governor of Barbados had set up a Council for the island. Some ten years later an elected House of Assembly was established, with twenty-two members, two representing each parish. Local administration at parish level became the responsibility of the vestry, a committee consisting of sixteen elected men. In this chapter we will look at the records of these bodies, as well as records relating to voters.

The Governor

The Governor was appointed by the Crown (i.e., the King or Queen in England) to represent its interests on the island. All bills passed by the Council and Assembly needed the Governor's signature before becoming law. In due course they were confirmed by the Crown. See Appendix 5 for a list of Governors from 1625–1966. The BML has a large folder of information on Governors, including biographical details for some of them.

The Council

The Council was made up of twelve members appointed by the Crown on the recommendation of the Governor. Members were usually prominent, wealthy merchants and planters.

The House of Assembly

The twenty-two members of the House of Assembly (two representing each parish) were elected by freeholders. Those eligible to vote and stand in elections to the House at the time it was established were white, Christian males, aged over twenty-one, citizens of Great Britain who owned at least ten acres of land or a house with an annual taxable value of £10.

Records of the Council and House of Assembly

If you have ancestors who served on the Council or House of Assembly, these will be of interest to you. Names of many other people are also included. Council minutes include lists of justices of the peace and jurors, details of petitions, probates of wills, appeals and grievances. House of Assembly minutes include wills proved, letters of administration applied for, liquor licenses issued and official appointments.

Transcripts of early Council minutes were made by Judge Nathaniel Lucas, a member of the Council. These are in two series:
1. Minutes of Council
2. Miscellaneous
Known as the *Lucas Manuscripts*, they cover the period 1653/4–1827 and are held on microfilm at the NLS. Extracts have been published in the JBMHS Vols. 9–17 and 24–27.

Original Council minutes and proceedings of the House of Assembly are held on microfilm at the NLS as follows:
*   Council 1836–1848
*   House of Assembly 1781–1848
*   Combined Council and House of Assembly records 1849–1866

Since 15 April 1867 an *Official Gazette* has been published, and its contents include the proceedings of the Council and House of Assembly. (For a few years prior to this, it was combined with various newspapers; see the "Newspapers" chapter for a listing.) The *Official Gazette* can be seen at:
*   NLS on microfilm, 1867–1914
*   NLS on their shelves, 1954 to date
*   BDA, 1871 to date, but note that early editions are in poor condition and it may not be possible to see them.

Lists of councilors, assemblymen and judges in 1679/80 are included in J.C. Hotten's *Original Lists of Persons of Quality...and Others Who Went from Great Britain to the American Plantations, 1600–1700* (BDA, BML).

The Parish

In 1629 the island was divided into six parishes, increasing to eleven in the early 1640s. Each parish had its own church, and a minister or rector was appointed. An administrative body for each parish was set up, known as the vestry, named after the room in which it met.

Freeholders of the parish annually selected sixteen of their number to serve as vestry members along with the rector of the parish. The various officers appointed included the churchwarden, sidesmen, constable, overseer of the poor and surveyor of the highways. Among their many duties the vestry was responsible for the upkeep of the church and the parish roads, for policing the parish, providing relief for the poor and for the collection of rents and taxes.

In 1959 the vestry system was abolished and replaced by city and district councils.

Records created at parish level are held at the BDA, with some microfilm copies at the BPL. Those of most interest to family historians are described here. Not all categories of record survive for all parishes, and the condition of the records varies. Some have been repaired; others are in poor condition and it may not be possible to see them. A full list of parish records and their condition (including some not described here) can be seen in the "Preliminary List 2," a black binder on the shelves of the BDA search room.

Contents of parish records

Vestry minutes
Parish business is documented here along with names of officers and other parish members who were involved in the running of the parish. People other than prominent members of the parish sometimes are featured, as this example shows:

St Michael 2 Feb 1756
That the Churchwarden do pay to Ann Butcher, widow, ten pounds per annum to be paid quarterly for the support of Lewis Loting an infant whose mother is dead and father run off.

Rate assessment books, rate books, levy books
These are records of those liable to pay local taxes and rates and are organized alphabetically by surname, or by street in some cases. They list owners and inhabitants along with property valuations or land acreage and the amount of tax due or paid.

Poor Law Guardian minute books
Parish residents who were in financial need applied for parish relief, and details were recorded in the minutes. Many names are mentioned, sometimes with an explanation of the circumstances and the amount of relief agreed.

Where to find parish records

The following table shows the records that can be seen at the BDA and copies on microfilm at the NLS. In addition:

- The BDA holds trade rate books for St Michael only, from 1910–1959

- The BML holds copies of the following vestry minutes, which can be seen depending on their condition:
    - St Michael, Mar 1655–Mar 1677, Jan 1743–Aug 1745, 1789–1805
    - St John, 1649–1699, 1792–1820, 25 Mar 1829–25 Mar 1863, Mar 1863–Oct 1884

The JBMHS has published extracts from some vestry minutes:

- St John from 1649–1674, Vol. 33: 32–49
- St John from 1674–1678, Vol. 37: 161–173
- St Michael from 1655–1757, Vols. 14–27

Parish records at the Barbados Department of Archives

Parish	Vestry minutes	Rate assessment books	Rate books	Levy books	Poor Law Guardian minute books
St Andrew	1902–1959 (on M/F at BDA & NLS)	1920–1959 with gaps	1918–1921, 1925–1930, 1932–1959		1928–1959 (on M/F at BDA & NLS)
Christ Church	1831–1859	1929–1930, 1937–1957	1905–1959		1906–1912, 1919–1959
St George	1806–1959 (on M/F at BDA & NLS)	1912–13, 1917–1923, 1925–1959	1891–1902, 1906–1914, 1918–1959		1903–1959 (on M/F at BDA & NLS)
St James	1873–1885 (on M/F at BDA & NLS), 1921–1959 with gaps	1920–24, 1927–28, 1945–1959	1916–1923, 1932–34, 1945–46, 1949–1959		1942–1959
St John	1649–1682, 1792–1820, 1896–1959	1944–46, 1948–1958	1940–1959		1939–1959
St Joseph	1896–1925 (on M/F at BDA & NLS)	1914, 1923–1931, 1937–39, 1945–1959	1905–1910, 1916–17, 1921–22, 1924–1959		1902–08, 1933–1942, 1946–1959
St Lucy	1846–1885 (on M/F at BDA & NLS), 1926–1958	1927–29, 1940–49 with gaps, 1949–1959	1934–1959		1953–58
St Michael	1678/9 to 1959 with gaps (early books in poor condition)		1843, 1847, 1851, 1852, 1858, 1862, 1869–1882 with gaps, 1887–1959	1686–1715, 1722–1729, 1749–1765, 1768–1810, 1823–1829, 1841–1844 with gaps.	
St Peter	1952–59	1932–1958	1932–1959		1954–1959
St Philip	1794–1959	1927–1956 with gaps	1874–1958 with gaps		1902–1959
St Thomas	1843–1884 (on M/F at BDA & NLS), 1902–1959	1923–1933, 1942–44	1920–1959		1933–1959

Other official records

Blue Books

The Blue Book is an annual Government publication of statistics and contains a detailed account of all the taxes and duties collected by the Government. Although dealing mainly with statistics, it contains much of value to the family historian looking for background information on individuals.

Taking the 1901 edition as an example, information to be found here includes a listing of members of the Council and Assembly along with their dates of appointment and other civil or military offices held. Names of those serving on administrative boards and in the civil establishment are listed, showing their office held, date of appointment and by whom appointed, and their annual salary. The list of officers is long and wide-ranging, including for example the chief clerk to the Treasury, warders at Glendairy Prison and the second master at Lodge School.

Pensions paid are listed with—for each pensioner—name, amount of pension, authority under which the pension was granted, date from which it was paid, service for which the pension was granted, amount of emolument, when last employed in public service, present age of pensioner and cause of retirement.

Blue Books can be seen, depending on their condition, at:
- BDA 1833–1947 (on microfilm 1839, 1841–42, 1870–1947)
- BML 1877–1929, early books in poor condition
- NLS 1833–1869 on microfilm

Commission records

The BDA holds a collection of commission records in their reference RB7/22 covering 1841–1860, and in RB7/23 covering 1861–1895. Each volume has an index at the front giving name, date of commission, office appointed to, and a page reference to the full entry.

A typical entry in the index is:
Watts, John Scantlebury, 8 Sep 1862, Second Clerk of the Customs Establishment P.51

Some other matters are dealt with in these volumes, including warrants to transfer prisoners to the lunatic asylum and free pardons granted to prisoners.

Voters registers

Registers of those eligible to vote can be of interest to researchers as they place ancestors at a certain social level and provide details of abode and, sometimes, occupations. Various franchise acts were passed in Barbados that defined people's eligibility to vote, be elected to public office or serve on juries. People not featuring in voters registers may have been resident on the island but not eligible for inclusion. We will look first at the records, then at the eligibility requirements.

Surviving voters registers are held at the BDA and cover 1867–1938, although many are "closed" and therefore unavailable due to their poor condition. The registers are organized by year, by parish, and then alphabetically by surname. These are typical entries describing the electors' eligibility to vote along with their place of residence:

1872, Parish of St Andrew
Greaves, Henry – Lands and Tenements – Cheltenham Plantation
Whitehead, John Benjamin – Lands and Tenements – adjoining
Boscobelle Plantation

The BDA also holds Registers of Electors for 1951, 1956–67 and 1969.

Some of the voters lists for early years have been published in issues of *The Barbados Almanac,* and these survive from as early as 1816. See the "Newspapers and directories" chapter for a listing.

The list of voters for Barbados in 1873 can be found in JBMHS 50: 154–165.

Messrs Greaves and Whitehead in the example above were eligible for inclusion in the register by virtue of their "lands and tenements." Until 1950 certain property and income requirements had to be met, and these varied over time.

Until 1831 the only people eligible to vote were white, Christian men aged over 21 who were citizens of Great Britain, owning at least ten acres of land or a house with an annual taxable value of £10. In 1831 the taxable house value was increased to £30, and for the first time Jews, free coloreds and free blacks could vote.

In 1844 the property qualifications changed to freeholders £12.16s.4d, occupiers (town dwellers only) £32.1s, ratepayers £3.4s.

In 1884 property qualifications changed again to annual taxable value —freeholders £5, occupiers £15 in the town and country, ratepayers in Bridgetown £2, rural rate payers £1. For the first time an income requirement was included based on workers in town and country with an annual income of £50 or more

From 1943 women were given the vote for the first time, on the same terms as men. The annual income requirement was reduced to £25; property requirements remained the same.

From 1950 property and income requirements were removed and all adults now qualified.

Further reading

Campbell, P.F. *The Barbados Vestries 1627–1700,* JBMHS 37: 35–56 and 174–196 (BDA, BML, NLS)

Phillips, Anthony D.C.V. *The Parliament of Barbados 1639–1989,* JBMHS 38: 422–451 (BDA, BML, NLS)

Chapter 16

Military records

To protect Barbados from foreign attack and internal unrest, a local militia was established soon after settlement and remained in existence until the end of 1868. From time to time, as the need arose, Imperial forces were sent from Britain and quartered on the island. In 1780 a permanent garrison was established, and this became the head-quarters of the British land forces in the Eastern Caribbean until 1905.

The death rate among the soldiers was very high, due more to disease than warfare. To offset this drain on manpower, from 1795 twelve West Indian regiments were raised locally. The troops were predominantly black, led by white officers. After the Imperial forces were withdrawn in 1905 the island's security again became the responsibility of a local militia. The Barbados Volunteer Force was formed in 1902 and renamed the Barbados Battalion at the start of the Second World War in 1939. In 1948 it was re-designated the Barbados Regiment, and in 1979 was incorporated into the newly formed Barbados Defence Force.

The militia

All owners of property and those with income above a certain level had to provide militiamen from their family or servants (or serve themselves). The service was given free and those providing militiamen had also to provide arms and equipment. There were officers with the rank of colonel, lieutenant-colonel, major, captain and lieutenant. There are no original records of the militia in Barbados, but some listings can be found in published sources.

In 1680 militia rolls were submitted to the Colonial Office in London. Five "regiments of foot" totaling 4,810 men and two "regiments of horse" totaling 778 were included. A full listing can be found on pages 99–212 of the following:

Brandow, James C. *Omitted Chapters from Hotten's Original List of Persons of Quality* (BDA, BML)

Barbadians were involved in the English settlement of Jamaica when Penn and Venables captured the island from the Spanish in 1655. Names can be found, in Volume 2, pages 208–215 and 251–256, under the heading *A particular list of persons paid their 1st months pay for their respective qualities under the command of General Venables in the West Indies, December 1654*, of the following:
Oliver, Vere Langford. *Caribbeana* 6 vols., (BDA, BML, NLS)

A list of officers in the militia in 1831 published in an 1832 almanac has been transcribed and reproduced in the JBMHS 17: 111–118 (BDA, BML, NLS).

A Return of Enrolments of Yeomanry in Several Parishes, June 1866 is a list of about 300 names, organized by parish and including date, name, age, residence and remarks. This is held at the BML in the Shilstone Collection, Vol. XVI.

The Imperial and local forces from 1780

Records of the British Army regiments that served in the Caribbean are kept in England. For more information on available military records see:

www.nationalarchives.gov.uk
and
Grannum, Guy. *Tracing Your West Indian Ancestors* (BDA, BML).

http://website.lineone.net/~bwir/regiments.htm
The website of the British West India Regiments. Note in particular correspondence concerning the purchase of slaves for enlistment into the regiments.

www.regiments.org
The website for land forces of Britain, the Empire and Commonwealth.

Sources in Barbados

Some soldiers who served in Barbados did not return home. Many died of tropical diseases; others married and had children and settled on the island. We will look at some sources where records of these might be found.

St Ann's Garrison records of baptism, marriage and burial

As we have already seen in the chapter dealing with records of baptism, marriage and burial, events relating to soldiers can be found in church records—Anglican and other denominations. Figure 4 on page 41 shows marriages conducted by the "Roman Catholic minister to HM Troops." However, some events took place at the Garrison, and separate records were kept for these. When searching for baptism, marriage and burial for military ancestors, you should check both sets of records.

The records for St Ann's Garrison are held at the BDA, and the procedure for accessing them is the same as for the church records described earlier. The Garrison records are indexed separately under RL1/84 baptism, RL1/85 marriage and RL1/86 burial. Garrison entries are at the end of the index following listings for non-conformists.

The years covered by these records and their contents are:

Baptism 1843–1886
Date of birth, place and date of baptism, name, parents' names, rank of father, officiating minister.

Marriage 1843–1861
Date, rank and name of soldier, condition (widower, bachelor), name of bride, condition (widow, spinster), place of marriage, 2 witnesses, officiating minister.

Burial 1862–1886
Date of burial, name and rank, age, country of origin, religion.

Advice on other ways to access the burial records is given below.

Note that this group of records is *not* included in the LDS Church IGI and its website.

The Barbados Military Cemetery

The Military Cemetery, situated at Needham's Point in St Michael (next to the Hilton Hotel), is well worth visiting. Maintained since 1975 by the Barbados Military Cemetery Association, it is attractive and beautifully kept and has some fascinating monumental inscriptions. It is assumed that burials took place there from 1780 but the earliest legible tombstone is dated 1820. The cemetery is still used for the burial of ex-servicemen and women and serving members of the Defence Force. A site plan and list of tombstones are kept in the cemetery's Memorial Building.

Other monuments are also located in the Garrison area. Descriptions of these other monuments and the names listed are given, along with the inscriptions in the Military Cemetery, in:

Gleadall, Mary E. *Monumental Inscriptions in the Barbados Military Cemetery* (BDA, BML)
The following are included with a full name index:
- Tombstones in the Barbados Military Cemetery 1820–2000 *
- Entries in the St Ann's Garrison burial register 1862–1886 *
- World Wars I & II Roll of Honor
- World Wars I & II Commonwealth War Graves in Barbados
- Monument standing in front of the Barbados Museum to members of the Royal York Rangers who fell in action in 1809–1810
- The Hurricane Memorial standing at Bush Hill in the Garrison area, to members of the 36th Regiment lost in the hurricane of 1831
- Memorial in St Matthias churchyard to *HMS Dauntless* victims of yellow fever in 1852
- "Biographies of a Few" who feature on the tombstones
- Lists of British Army units, military service units and naval ships recorded on headstones

* These can also be seen on the Internet at **www.tombstones.bb**.

Leverick's Directory of Barbados 1921 (BDA, BML)
Hundreds of names of those who served in WWI are included in an article, *Our Part in the Great War*.

The *Official Gazette*
The *Gazette* publishes details of commissioned officers. See the "Island administration" chapter for more information.

St Ann's Garrison archives
Records of local forces for the 20th century to the present day are kept in the archives of St Ann's Garrison. However, records before 1950 were destroyed, with the exception of the *Commissions in the Local Forces Oath Book* for the period 23 March 1936 to 1960. The archives are not open to the public but the archivist will answer questions, at his discretion. He can be contacted at St Ann's Garrison, St Michael, Barbados.

Internet sources

www.cwgc.org
The Commonwealth War Graves Commission's *Debt of Honour Register* lists the men and women of the Commonwealth forces who died during the two world wars and the cemeteries and memorials where they are commemorated.

A successful search for a name will reveal the following information: name, nationality, rank, regiment, unit, date of death, service number, casualty type, cemetery and grave/memorial reference. Sometimes additional information is given, such as names of the next of kin.

Further reading

Alleyne, Warren. *Barbados at War 1939–1945: A Historical Account* (BDA, BML, NLS)

Alleyne, Warren, and Jill Sheppard. *The Barbados Garrison and its Buildings* (BDA, BML, NLS)

Campbell, P.F. *The Barbados Militia 1627–1815,* JBMHS 35: 103–119 (BDA, BML, NLS)

Dyde, Brian. *The Empty Sleeve: The Story of the West India Regiments of the British Army* (BDA, BML, NLS)

Chapter 17

Immigration and emigration

From the earliest days of settlement by the English, immigrants arrived in Barbados in large numbers in search of land and work. Fortunes were to be made by those able to invest in land. Indentured servants came from England, Scotland and Ireland in the hope of being rewarded with a piece of land at the end of their contract; few were, and many moved on to seek their fortunes elsewhere. Political rebels were dispatched to the colonies instead of being hanged, and Barbados received many of these, particularly after the Monmouth rebellion of 1685 and the Jacobite rebellion of 1745–46. Irish people were transported to the island following the wars in the 1640s and 1650s.

By the 1650s large numbers of African slaves were providing much of the labor force needed for the growing sugar industry. Migration from Barbados to other Caribbean islands, North America and other destinations began in the 17th century and continued throughout subsequent centuries.

When an ancestor is found in the records of Barbados, the next questions are, "Why did he/she come to Barbados, where from and when?" These are not easy questions to answer, since very few records of arrivals and departures are held in Barbados, and those that exist relate mostly to cargoes rather than people. In this chapter we will look at the few remaining records on the island and also the large number of published sources, which provide valuable information for researchers.

Records at the Barbados Department of Archives

In the 19th and 20th centuries numerous people emigrated but, since many of them left on their own initiative and at their own expense, they do not appear in any records. The following records are the few exceptions to this.

Emigrants' registers to Panama and other destinations 1906–1912

Nearly 20,000 people emigrated to Panama starting in the 1850s, the majority going between 1905 and 1913 to work on the Panama Canal project. Some of these are listed in the District A Emigrants Registers (which include names from all parishes) covering 1906–1912, in 3 volumes. These are organized alphabetically by surname with the following columns:

- Name of emigrant
- Age
- Father and mother's name (often other family names given instead)
- Residence (usually area and parish are given)
- Destination—mostly Panama
- Emigration agent
- Contractor
- Period of contract (for Panama, usually 500 days)

Emigrants' register to Curaçao and other destinations 1941–1948

This register includes about a thousand names of people going mainly to Curaçao, with some to Canada, USA, Venezuela and other Caribbean islands. Names are listed alphabetically, along with occupation and destination.

Register of Bonds to Depart the Island 1834/5

BDA Ref: RB9/2/4. About 500 names are listed, along with parish of residence and destination.

Bonds for Tickets to Depart the Island 21 March 1766–12 April 1766

BDA Ref: RB9/2/2. Only eleven items survive. Each document gives the name and parish of the person traveling and those of the two people acting as surety. See Appendix 6 for a full listing of the thirty-one people named in these documents.

Published Sources

Some of the records held in the UK and other places relating to emigration to and from Barbados have been transcribed and published. It is well worth searching these for the names you are interested in. Most can be seen on the shelves of the BML and the BDA. Those that cannot are published by the Genealogical Publishing Company and Clearfield Company (see "Bibliography" for details) and are available from **www.genealogical.com**, some on CD-ROM as well as in book form. The publications listed here relate to the US and Caribbean mainly, but in all cases names relating to Barbados are included, together with a names index.

Baldwin, Agnes Leland, *First Settlers of South Carolina* *1670–1680* **(BDA, BML)**
Sources are taken from original records in London and South Carolina. The listing includes names, others in the family, the town settled in, occupation and title, servants and slaves, place of origin (many from Barbados), date of arrival.

Chandler, M.J. *Emigrants from Britain to the Colonies of America and the West Indies,* JBMHS 36: 28–43 **(BDA, BML, NLS)**
This includes a list of 410 indentured servants traveling in the years 1682–1686 from an original list at the Guildhall Library, London.

Coldham, Peter Wilson. *The Complete Book of Emigrants in* *4 volumes 1607–1776*
• Volume 1: 1607–1660
• Volume 2: 1661–1699
• Volume 3: 1700–1750
• Volume 4: 1751–1776
There are also two related volumes:
Coldham, Peter Wilson. *The Complete Book of Emigrants in Bondage 1614–1775*
Coldham, Peter Wilson. *Supplement to The Complete Book of Emigrants in Bondage 1614–1775*
The above six books contain a total of about 140,000 names, mostly people heading for the US but many for Barbados. Records in England were used, including port books, shipping registers, apprenticeship lists, Treasury and Chancery records and records of forced transportation and exile. The six books combined are available on CD-ROM.

Coldham, Peter Wilson. *English Convicts in Colonial America* *Vol. I Middlesex 1617–1775* **(BDA, BML)**
This listing is taken from various primary sources in London plus some secondary sources. Most relate to US-bound convicts but some went to Barbados. For example:
Gardner, Elizabeth, pleaded transportation to Barbados, Jan. 1694.

Coldham, Peter Wilson. *The Bristol Registers of Servants Sent to Foreign Plantations 1654–1686*
This is a listing of indentured servants mainly from the West Country, the West Midlands and Wales, showing names of servants, masters,

places of origin and ships. The list is also in JBMHS Vols. 14–19 (BDA, BML, NLS).

Darnell Davis, N. *Cavaliers & Roundheads of Barbados 1650–1652* (BDA, BML)

This publication includes on pages 42–43 the names of those on board Captain Powell's ship *The Peter*, which arrived in Barbados in 1627.

Dobson, David. *Scots in the West Indies 1707–1857*

The contents are taken from a variety of sources in archives in Scotland, England and Denmark as well as numerous publications. The information given for each person varies and may include occupation, education and parents' names as well as name, island inhabited and date.

Dobson, David. *The Original Scots Colonists of Early America, Caribbean supplement 1611–1707*

Numerous primary and secondary sources in the UK and US were used to compile this book. There is some overlap with Hotten's *Original Lists* (see next page), as this was used as a source.

Dobson, David. *Directory of Scots Banished to the American Plantations 1650–1775* (BML)

Sources used include records of the Privy Council of Scotland, Treasury and state papers, prison records and various published works. A large number relate to those banished to the plantations for their part in the Jacobite rebellion of 1745. The following is a typical entry:

GRANT Peter, 24, Fiddler. Glen Urquhart. Jacobite in Glengarry's Regiment. Prisoner at Inverness, ship and Medway. Transported from London to Barbados or Jamaica by Samuel Smith 31 March 1747.

Dobson, David. *Barbados and Scotland, Links 1627–1877* (BML)

Sources in Scotland, England, the Netherlands, the US and many in Barbados were drawn on for this book. About 2,500 Scots and their descendants who arrived in Barbados in the 17th and 18th centuries are included. For most the following is recorded: name, date/place of birth, baptism, marriage, death, name of spouse or parents. For some, additional details are given such as occupation, reason for transportation, ship, religious or political persuasion and other miscellaneous information.

Fothergill, Gerald. *Emigrant Ministers to America 1690–1811* (BML).

A bounty of £20 was paid to ministers and schoolmasters who went to the colonies. This listing is taken from records held in London and includes destination, date, sometimes family information and abode in the UK. It mainly relates to the US but there are some entries for Barbados.

Ghirelli, Michael. *A List of Emigrants from England to America 1682–1692* **(BDA, BML)**
The listing includes the names of 125 people bound for Barbados. The entries are transcribed from the Lord Mayor's Waiting Books at the City of London Record Office. These list persons who wished to emigrate but lacked the money to do so. In most cases they were shipped out by sea captains or agents who collected fees from the employer in the colonies. Some or all of the following information is given: name, age, parentage, place of origin, occupation and for indentured servants sometimes the length of service and who they were bonded to.

Hotten, J.C. *Original Lists of Persons of Quality...and Others Who Went from Great Britain to the American Plantations, 1600–1700* **(BDA, BML)**
This important publication by Hotten includes:
• Passenger lists, some for ships heading to Barbados
• A list of "convicted rebels" from the Monmouth Rebellion in 1685, many heading for Barbados
• Tickets granted to emigrants from Barbados to New England, Carolina, Virginia, New York, Antigua, Jamaica, Newfoundland and other places, 1678–79. This list is also in the JBMHS 1: 155–180 (BDA, BML, NLS).

Kaminkow, Jack & Marion. *Original Lists of Emigrants in Bondage from London to the American Colonies 1719–1744* **(BDA)**
These are records extracted from the Treasury Money Books. The Treasury paid expenses relating to those being transported. People listed here are mainly from London, Surrey, Middlesex, Kent, Sussex, Hertfordshire and Buckinghamshire. Names are listed alphabetically along with a reference to further information, typically place of origin, destination, ship, captain and date.

McDonnell, Frances. *Highland Jacobites 1745* **(BML)**
Taken from records in London and Edinburgh the list includes some persons headed for Barbados as well as other Caribbean islands. The usual information given is name, rank, dates of service and unit (if military), and frequently the subject's date and place of imprisonment, date and place of transportation, name of vessel and date of arrival.

Nicholson, Cregoe D.P. *Some Early Emigrants to America and Early Emigrants to America from Liverpool* **(BDA)**
This listing was originally transcribed in 1948 and published in the *Genealogists' Magazine*. The information is taken from records held in Middlesex Guildhall, London, of indentures of "persons willing to serve in the plantations," and includes name, age, occupation, place of origin, ship, person assigned to, and date.

Wareing, John. *Emigrants to America: Indentured Servants Recruited in London 1718–1733* **(BML)**
Most people listed were bound for the US or Jamaica; forty-three relate to Barbados. The information is extracted from a register, held at the Record Office of the Corporation of London, of people who voluntarily contracted to go to plantations in the colonies. It includes names, the name of the emigration agent, destination and date.

Websites

www.ellisisland.org
This website includes records of 25 million immigrant passengers and crew passing through Ellis Island, the Port of New York, from 1892–1924. It can be searched by surname and is very useful for researching those who went from Barbados to the USA. The results of a surname search will include name, age on arrival, year of arrival and place of residence prior to arrival in the US. By registering with the site (free of charge) it is possible to see more details, including ethnicity, last place of residence, date of arrival, gender, marital status, ship of travel and port of departure.

Other sources

The Barbados Museum Library holds folders of information on the Irish-Barbados connection and the Scottish-Barbados connection. Another collection covers the "redlegs," indentured servants who fell on hard times (the name deriving from their sunburned legs) and were other-wise known as "poor whites."

A regular feature in old Barbados newspapers was headed:

"Secretary's Office. The following is a list of persons who intend leaving the island as well as those who have quitted on leaving security."
To prevent servants and debtors fleeing the island, all those planning to leave were required to register at the Colonial Secretary's Office three weeks in advance. These listings in the newspapers would be

worth checking; see the "Newspapers" chapter for more information on dates available.

Further Reading

Alleyne, Warren, and Henry Fraser. *The Barbados-Carolina Connection* (BDA, BML, NLS)

Campbell, P.F. *The Adventures of a Monmouth Rebel,* JBMHS 35: 144–152 (BDA, BML, NLS)

D'Arcy McGee. Thomas, *A History of the Irish Settlers in North America*

Dobson, David. *Scottish Emigration to Colonial America, 1607–1785*

Foster, Andrea C.A. *Barbadian Emigration to Curacao 1930–1960,* JBMHS 38: 286–314 (BDA, BML, NLS)

Maughan, Basil. *Some aspects of Barbadian Emigration to Cuba 1919–1935,* JBMHS 37: 239–276 (BDA, BML, NLS)

Newton, Velma. *Recruiting West Indian Labourers for the Panama Canal & Railroad Construction Projects 1850–1914,* JBMHS 37: 9–19 (BDA, BML, NLS)

Newton, Velma. *The Silver Men: West Indian Labour Migration to Panama 1850–1914* (BDA, BML, NLS)

O'Callaghan, Sean. *To Hell or Barbados: The Ethnic Cleansing of Ireland* (BML)

Price, Edward T. *The "Redlegs" of Barbados,* JBMHS 29: 47–52 (BDA, BML, NLS)

Roberts, G.W. *Emigration From the Island of Barbados* (BML)

Sheppard, Jill. *The "Redlegs" of Barbados: Their Origins and History* (BDA, BML, NLS)

Watson, Karl. *"The Barbadians Endeavour to Rule All." A socio-political commentary on Barbados/Carolinas relationship in the Seventeenth Century,* JBMHS 43: 78–95 (BDA, BML, NLS)

Chapter 18

Slave records

Genealogical research for black families back to the emancipation of slaves in 1834 proceeds in the same way as for white families. In both cases family members can provide information and family documents and memorabilia can be collected. Both white and black families registered birth and death and had other family events recorded in church records and cemeteries. Some will have featured in the other records we have covered so far. The search is easier for some black families during this period, just as it is for some whites, for the simple reason that families with wealth, property and position are more frequently documented. As we have discussed before, the links for some families are simply not there, and the trail goes cold after two or three generations. For those with black ancestry who have been successful in tracing back several generations, this chapter describes the next steps.

Research becomes more difficult in the years before 1834 when most black people were held in slavery. In this chapter we will look at the two main sources of data on slaves. If you have discovered that your ancestors were free at the time of emancipation, you should continue your research in the records you have already used as well as in those described here.

There are two important points to bear in mind when using these records. Firstly, slaves, as the property of their owners, were recorded under their owners' names, not their own. It is therefore essential to know to whom they belonged at this point. Secondly, most slaves did not have surnames, making it difficult to find them in the records. The name of the owner can help here to distinguish one "William" or "Sarah" from another.

Much has been written about slaves and slavery in Barbados, and the "Further reading" for this chapter lists books written by experts on the subject. These are useful if you would like to know more about the lives of your slave ancestors. Included on the list are some titles relating to slave naming. Slaves were often denied surnames as they were the property of their owner and had no legal connection with their father. In the years following emancipation (in some cases many years later), freed slaves who had not previously had surnames adopted them. Possible sources of the name include the surname of the owner, the surname of the father (who may also have been the owner), the surname of a previous owner, the name of a plantation or a name simply chosen at random. Some slaves with two names adopted the second as their surname, for example Edward Thomas. There are other theories and much debate on the subject. See "Further reading."

Slave registers

Following the abolition of the slave trade between Africa and the British colonies in 1807 a system was needed to keep a check on slave ownership. Between 1817 and emancipation in 1834, registers of slaves were kept in Barbados and copies were forwarded to the Colonial Office in London. These records survive at the National Archives in London in their reference T71, and microfilm copies can be seen in Barbados at the Library of the University of the West Indies, Cave Hill campus.

Returns were made in 1817, 1820, 1823, 1826, 1829, 1832 and 1834.

Indexes to the registers

Indexes are organized by parish and then by the first letter of slave owners' surnames. The number of slaves owned is given along with the volume and page number of the register where the full entry can be found.

Contents of the registers

The contents described here vary. Some slave owners were non-white; in the registers FM stands for "free mulatto" and FN for "free negro."

1817, 1820
For these years a full listing of slaves is given. Each entry in the register gives the name of the slave owner along with the name of the plantation (if he had one—many were small households). The slaves are then listed in columns headed: name, sex, color, employment (e.g. watchman, gardener, carter, mason, groom), age, country (of birth, usually Africa or Barbados, with a few exceptions).

BDA: Barbados Department of Archives; BML: Barbados Museum Library

1823, 1826, 1829, 1832
Only increases and decreases in the number of slaves owned are recorded for these years. If a slave remained with the same owner for the whole of the year in question, he or she will not appear in the registers.

As before, each entry gives the name of the slave owner and plantation (if applicable). The increase column shows slaves born, purchased, received by gift or inherited (and in these cases from whom). The decrease column shows those who have died, been sold or given as gifts (and to whom), or sent off the island. In all cases the slaves are named and their age, color and country of origin are given.

1834
A full listing is given, as for 1817 and 1820, but occupations are described simply as laborer or domestic. Reasons for increase and decrease are included.

Accessing the records

Contact details for the University of the West Indies (UWI) can be found in the "List of archives" chapter, and the University will need advance notice of your visit.

The microfilms at the UWI Library are labeled with the references of the National Archives, London, as shown in this table:

Year	Register volumes	Indexes
1817	T71/ 520-522	T71/ 523
1820	T71/ 524-527	T71/ 528
1823	T71/ 529-532	T71/ 533
1826	T71/ 534-538	T71/ 539
1829	T71/ 540-545	T71/ 546
1832	T71/ 547-551	T71/ 552
1834	T71/ 553-564	T71/ 565

The name of the slave owner is essential to narrow down the search. The register for 1817, for example, lists the names of 77,493 slaves, so browsing through in the hope of finding one particular slave is not a practical option.

The first step is to request the index for the year you are interested in.

As an example we will look for this married couple just before they were granted their freedom in 1834.

Marriage
Christ Church 13 Oct 1832
Frank Will & Fanny, slaves of George Donovan
Officiating minister: J.H. Orderson
Witness: Thomas L. Ruck
BDA Ref: RL1/20/220

To check for the slave owner, George Donovan of Christ Church in 1834, we need index T71/565. The index tells us that he owns 88 slaves and refers us to page 91 in the third volume. There are twelve volumes for 1834 numbered 553 to 564, and so the third is number 555. We now need to request the microfilm for T71/555. The entry starting on page 91 gives us the following information about the two slaves named Fanny and Frank Will.

Slave Register
March 1834
Return of slaves owned by George Donovan of Christ Church Parish
88 slaves listed (38 males, 50 females) including:
Fanny aged 29, coloured, Barbadian, domestic
Frank Will aged 29, black, Barbadian, labourer
Ref: T71/555/91&92

This example illustrates one of the problems in using these records. We know from the church record that Fanny and Frank Will were married. In the slave register there are separate lists of male and female slaves with no indication of relationships, so their connection is not shown. There could have been a child of theirs on the list and no doubt other family groups. Even the registers for 1823–32 listing increases and decreases do not give the parentage of the slave additions due to birth or any relationships for slaves who died. The task may be easier where the number of slaves owned was small. In most cases then, while it may be possible to trace the whereabouts of a slave through the slave registers, these are not so helpful in building the family tree. Used in conjunction with the church records of baptism, marriage and burial you may have more success, particularly as slaves were recorded in larger numbers during this period.

The slave registers are also worth consulting for slave-owning ancestors. They give an indication of a person's wealth and in some cases the name of plantations owned. The increase and decrease columns show change of ownership through inheritance and marriage (a woman's slaves became her husband's on marriage), and names may be mentioned. Slaves owned by minors were registered in the names of their guardians. After a slave owner died, but before his will was proven, he was listed as "deceased," which can help in establishing a date of death.

Manumission records

These are documents granting freedom to slaves. The Emancipation Act granted freedom to all slaves in 1834. However, prior to the Act, some owners chose to grant freedom to individual slaves anyway, for a number of reasons. Illegitimate children of "mixed" relationships between slaves and free people were often manumitted. Some slaves were given the opportunity to buy their freedom, and others were freed in their owner's will. A slave who had served his or her owner well for many years may have been rewarded with manumission.

Although the freeing of slaves increased substantially in the years leading up to emancipation, this was not an entirely new practice; slaves were being freed—for reasons such as those given above— many years before emancipation.

To prevent irresponsible owners from granting freedom to old slaves who were no longer able to work, effectively "dumping" them, an act was passed in 1739 requiring owners to pay £50 to the vestry for every slave freed. The vestry then paid the ex-slave a pension. Names of the parties involved can be found in the vestry records, which are discussed in the "Island administration" chapter. An attempt was made to control the number of slaves being manumitted when a new act was passed in 1801 increasing manumission fees to £300 for men and £200 for women; this came into force in 1808. It did not reduce manumissions overall but did increase the number of slaves manu- mitted in England at the Lord Mayor's Office in London (and other mayors' offices around the country). No fees were payable in England, and the manumission documents were returned to Barbados where they were regarded as valid. In 1816 another act was passed reducing the fees back to £50. Records for this entire period can be seen in Barbados.

Manumission records are held at the BDA and include some very helpful information for research into slave and slave-owning families. To research a slave, the owner's name will be needed, as all records are indexed by owner. Some manumission records are in separate volumes and others are included in the deeds record books. We will look at each of these separately.

Manumission record books at the BDA

There are four volumes of manumissions, reference RB7/24–27. The first three are indexed by the slave owner's name with the name of his slave(s) alongside. The index to RB7/27 is not available for viewing due to its poor condition. RB7/26 and 27 are collections of printed forms with handwritten individual details. RB7/24 and 25 are handwritten volumes, which include some slave sales.

Deed record books at the BDA

A significant number of manumissions are recorded in the deeds record books, particularly in the early 19th century. For example, a check in the original deeds index for the letter C (surname of owner) from 1814–1833 revealed more than 90 manumissions for that letter alone. A difficulty in using these records is that the recopied deeds (unlike the original deeds) do not list the type of document in the index. So it is not possible to establish from the index which deeds are manumissions. See the "Deeds" chapter for more information on using these records.

Contents of manumission records

The following extracts are typical of the information given. London Bourne, the well-known black Bridgetown merchant, recorded here as a slave owner, is a reminder that not all slave owners were white:

London Bourne of the parish of St Michael manumitted a certain black slave named Molly Hamden Bourne. 9 May 1832
BDA Ref: RB7/26/65

Sarah Agard of the parish of St Michael manumitted her coloured male slave named Horatio Bath Agard. 1 Apr. 1833
BDA Ref: RB7/27/85

Maria Hollingsworth and Agnes Ann Hollingsworth of the parish of St Michael manumitted a certain black woman slave named Diana and her two coloured sons James and Tom (men). 21 Feb. 1833
BDA Ref: RB7/27/64

Ann Pilgrim of the parish of St Philip manumitted Kitty Ann Young, Samuel Crawford, Sarah Margaret Crawford and John Clement Crawford. 13 Mar. 1833
BDA Ref: RB7/27/78

Some records help with the family relationships of slave owners and their location in England.

Reverend Charles Kingsley of Barnack in the county of Northamptonshire and Mary his wife, daughter of the Honourable Nathan Lucas late of the island of Barbados and Mary his wife manumitted two female slaves Sally and Mary James otherwise called Mary Adamson. 24 Oct 1828
BDA Ref: RB7/24/273

A record like this next one can cause confusion when searching the index for a slave. Only the first-named slave, Margaret Ann, appears in the index (alongside her owner's name), so a search for Mary Wood, for example, would draw a blank.

Margaret Ann Beckles formerly of the Bay Estate near Bridge Town in the island of Barbados but now of the Gloucester Lodge, Old Brompton in the county of Middlesex spinster appointed the Honourable John Alleyne Beckles of Bay Estate and William Gill Esquire of Bridge Town to act as attorneys re the manumission of Margaret Ann (needlewoman), John Edward, William Butler, Mary Wood, Sarah Jane, Elizabeth Christian*. 7 Aug 1828
BDA Ref: RB7/25/43
(*All these slaves were described as colored and Barbadian.)

Confusion could occur when looking for this next record, as Samuel Hinds appears in the index, not the (now deceased) owner, James Crichlow Trotman:

The Honourable Samuel Hinds of the parish of St Michael Warden of the parochial church of the said parish of St Michael acting for James Crichlow Trotman late of this island Esquire, deceased in his will of 31 May 1809 desired to be manumitted a mulatto girl named Sarah Eliza daughter of Mary Ann Trotman commonly called Molly Ann Trotman, free mulatto woman.
BDA Ref: RB1/266/90

As these examples show, the key piece of information you will need to find a particular record is the name of the slave owner. If this is listed in the index the search should run smoothly. In some cases a different name is indexed (attorney or executor for example), as we have already seen. Another example where this problem arises is during the period 1808 to 1816 (described earlier) when most manumissions were executed in England to avoid exorbitant fees. Some "owners" appearing frequently during this period are in fact agents acting for slave owners on the island.

Further reading

Beckles, Hilary. *Black Rebellion in Barbados: The Struggle Against Slavery 1627–1838* (BDA, BML, NLS)

Beckles, Hilary. *Bussa: The 1816 Barbados Revolution* (BDA, BML, NLS)

Dunn, Richard S. *Sugar & Slaves: The Rise of the Planter Class in the English West Indies, 1624–1713* (BDA, BML, NLS)

Handler, Jerome S. *The Unappropriated People: Freedmen in the Slave Society of Barbados* (BDA, BML, NLS)

Handler, Jerome S. *Plantation Slavery in Barbados: An Archaeological & Historical Investigation* (BDA, BML, NLS)

Handler, Jerome S., and JoAnn Jacoby. *Slave Names and Naming in Barbados 1650–1830* (BDA, BML)

Salazar, L.E. *Love Child: A Genealogist's Guide to the Social History of Barbados* (BDA, BML, NLS)

Watson, Karl. *A Kind of Right to be Idle: Old Doll Matriarch of Newton Plantation* (BDA, BML, NLS)

Welch, Pedro L.V., with Richard A. Goodridge. *"Red" & Black over White: Free Coloured Women in Pre-Emancipation Barbados* (BDA, BML, NLS)

Welch, Pedro L.V. *Slave Society in the City: Bridgetown Barbados 1680–1834* (BDA, BML, NLS)

Welch, Pedro L.V. *"What's in a Name?" From Slavery to Freedom in Barbados* (BDA)

Chapter 19

DNA

According to James Watson, co-discoverer of DNA's double-helical structure, DNA (deoxyribonucleic acid) holds the key to the nature of all living things. In his book *DNA: The Secret of Life*, Professor Watson says: "It stores the hereditary information that is passed on from one generation to the next, and it orchestrates the incredibly complex world of the cell." So on the face of it, DNA information should be a valuable source for family historians. However, like so many sources available to us, it is not without its problems. This book is about physical records, and it is not the intention of this chapter to do any more than give a brief introduction to this complex subject and suggest where else to go for further information.

Background

In the 1980s people realized the potential of DNA testing for family history research and it is now sometimes used to supplement genealogical information derived from traditional sources. It is important to appreciate, however, that while the technique is good at revealing the existence or absence of a match between two results, in its current form DNA testing cannot definitively identify your ancestor.

Y chromosome DNA testing

At conception, everyone receives one chromosome from their mother and one from their father. The one from the mother is always an X chromosome and the one from the father may be either X or Y. This is what determines the sex of the child; girls have two X chromosomes and boys have one X and one Y.

A man inherits his Y chromosome from his father, who will have inherited it from his father and so on back through time. About once in every 20 generations however, the Y chromosome undergoes a change (or "mutation"), so not all men have exactly the same Y chromosome DNA. In other words, the greater the resemblance between two Y chromosome DNA results, the greater the likelihood that the individuals concerned are related.

Given that surnames are usually passed down via the male line, Y chromosome DNA results can be used by family historians in conjuncttion with research on a particular surname.

Mitochondrial DNA (mtDNA) testing

Mitochondrial DNA is always inherited from the mother, so rather like Y chromosome DNA for men, there is a link to the distant past, but this time passed down via the maternal line. Because mtDNA only mutates about once in every 500 generations it is the test of choice when trying to trace "deep ancestry"—i.e., identifying likely geographical origins. This is a test increasingly being used by African Americans interested in identifying the country of origin of their ancestors.

Benefits, problems and potential of DNA testing

The results of a DNA test will contain a lot of scientific data, which can be difficult for the layman to interpret and use. However, by comparing two or more sets of results you can begin to see if there might be a relationship between individuals or groups of people, or be able to confirm absolutely that there is no such relationship.

Sometimes a result will tell you little more than the broad geographical area from which your ancestors came. For example, the results of an mtDNA test for a black Barbadian, conducted as a test case for this book, simply told her that her ancestors were from Africa. In the longer term, it may be that further refinements in DNA testing and the establishment of larger, more comprehensive databases could improve the usefulness of such tests to family history research.

There are currently no incontrovertible tests for establishing member-ship of ethnic or tribal groups, but research in this area continues. If this is an area of interest to you, it is worth looking for up-to-date information from the websites on the next page.

Arranging a DNA test and the results

There are now several companies offering DNA tests, and most of these are in the United States. Some websites are given on the next page, and more detailed descriptions of tests can be found here. The current cost of DNA tests is around US$150 to US$350.

BDA: Barbados Department of Archives; BML: Barbados Museum Library

On request a company will send you a testing kit, which will include some small cotton wool swabs (like Q-Tips or cotton buds). These are used to collect cell samples from the inside of the mouth, which are then sent back to the company for analysis.

The results of the analysis will be a data sheet showing the makeup of the DNA and possibly a world map showing where people with similar DNA originated. Sometimes the company will be able to tell you of a match, either with a group of people on their database, or with specific individuals. If the individuals have agreed to have their personal details passed on, you will be given information that will enable you to make contact with them.

Further reading

Pomery, Chris. *DNA and Family History*
This book has an accompanying website:
www.dnaandfamilyhistory.com

Sykes, Bryan. *The Seven Daughters of Eve*

Companies that do DNA testing

www.africanancestry.com

www.dnaheritage.com

www.familytreedna.com

www.relativegenetics.com

Appendix 1

Timeline of principal records in Barbados available to researchers

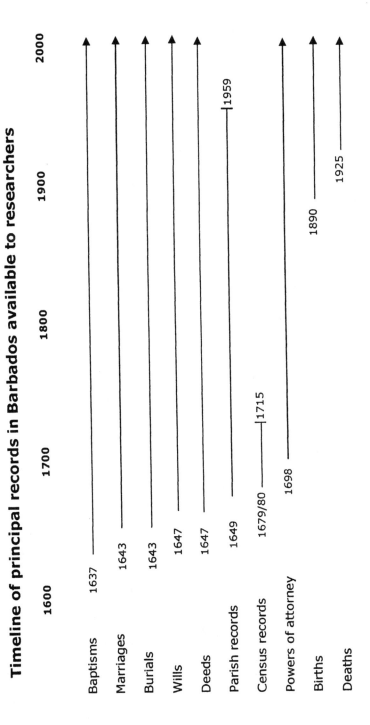

	1600	1700	1800	1900	2000
Baptisms	1637				
Marriages	1643				
Burials	1643				
Wills	1647				
Deeds	1647				
Parish records	1649				
Census records	1679/80 ——— 1715				
Powers of attorney		1698			
Births				1890	
Deaths				1925	
				1959	

Appendix 2

Worksheets for research in the records of baptism, marriage and burial (pp. 133-135)

Baptism Records

Family Name .... Period Covered ....

BDA ref No.	Parish *	Year	Date of Baptism	Date of Birth	Name	Parents' Names	Abode	Trade, profession, rank etc (of father)	Where event held and any other information

* X Christ Church; P St Philip; M St Michael; S St James; O St Joseph; T St Thomas; L St Lucy; E St Peter; G St George; J St John; A St Andrew

Marriage Records

Family Name ....   **Period Covered** ....

BDA Ref No.	Parish *	Year	Date of Marriage	Names	Age	Marital State	Occupations	Abode	Names and occupations of fathers	Where event held and any other information

* X Christ Church; P St Philip; M St Michael; S St James; O St Joseph; T St Thomas; L St Lucy; E St Peter; G St George; J St John; A St Andrew

Burial Records

Family Name .... **Period Covered** ....

BDA Ref No.	Parish *	Year	Date of Burial	Name	Age	Abode	Trade, Profession, Rank etc	Place of Birth	Where event held and any other Information

* X Christ Church; P St Philip; M St Michael; S St James; O St Joseph; T St Thomas; L St Lucy; E St Peter; G St George; J St John; A St Andrew

Appendix 3

Gaps in baptism and marriage records 1637–1800, as noted by Joanne McRee Sanders in *Barbados Records*

Parish	Baptism	Marriage
Christ Church	1720 Jan–Nov: no entries 1725 Feb–Dec: no entries 24 Mar 1732 to 29 Mar 1735: no entries 13 Nov 1748 to Oct 1751: no entries	21 Dec 1786 to 24 Dec 1795: no entries
St James	1702: no entries 20 Nov 1746 to 4 Apr 1751: no entries	No omissions noted
St John	Records start after 1800 and are therefore beyond the scope of Mrs Sanders' book	Oct 1672–Oct 1682: no entries 1701–1715: no entries 1690, 1691, 1726, 1727: no entries 1794–1817: no entries Mrs Sanders comments that these missing years account for approximately 25% of marriages for the period 1657–1800
St Joseph	All years are represented although some are sparse	1764, 1765, 1771, 1791, 1797: no entries, however Mrs Sanders comments that marriages allocated to other years might belong to these years; the dates in the original register are in poor condition, causing confusion
St Lucy	Reference to missing data but no dates given	Reference to difficulty in determining the extent of missing entries
St Michael	No omissions noted	Nov 1650–Nov 1652: no entries Jul 1653–Aug 1654: some entries missing 12 Oct 1659 to 14 Aug 1664: only 3 marriages recorded
St Peter	Since the surviving baptism and marriage records for this parish begin in 1779 the numbers included are small, and few if any entries are missing for this period	
St Philip	All imperfect before 1757 1658, 1659, 1669–1671, 1706–1708, 1748, 1750–1752, 1754, 1755: no entries	1689, 1690, 1739–1741: no entries 1754–1760: dates of marriages not recorded
St Thomas	1731, 1732, 1764–1766: no entries	1763–1766: no entries
St Andrew	The surviving baptism and marriage records for these parishes begin after 1800 and therefore fall outside the time covered by Mrs Sanders' book	
St George		

Appendix 4

**Names included in:
Hughes, Ronald. *The Barbadian Sugar Magnates
1643–1783: Some Jottings*, JBMHS 35: 211–222**

Adams Alleyne Applewhaite Archer Armstrong Atkins

Barwicke Bell Birney Bond Boxill Boyce Brevitor Briggs

Challenor Chandler Clarke Cleland Codrington Colleton Connell Crowe

Davers Dottin Drax Dudley Duke

Edney Estwicke Evans

Farmer Forde Forstall Fortescue Frere Fretwell

Gibbes Gibson Greaves Grey Griffith Guy

Hanson Hawley Hawtaine Holder Holdip Hooper Hothersall Howell
Humphrey Husbands

Kendall Kingsland

Lambert Lascelles Leacock Lear Legard Lillington Littleton Lowther

Mason Maycock Middleton Molineux

Osborne

Pace Paynter Peers Pile Pilgrim Pinder Pollard

Rawdon Reece Rous

Sandiford Searle Skeete Standfast Swann

Terrill Thomas Thornhill

Walduck Walker Walrond Walter Wardall Weekes Wheeler Willoughby
Worsam

Yeamans Yearwood

Appendix 5

Governors of Barbados from settlement in 1627 to independence in 1966

John Powell	1627
Charles Wolverston	1628
Sir William Tufton, Bart.	1629
Henry Hawley	1630
Sir Henry Hunks	1640
Philip Bell	1641
Francis Lord Willoughby	1650
Sir George Ayscue	1652
Daniel Searle	1652
Thomas Modyford	1660
Francis, Lord Willoughby	1663
Henry Willoughby	1666 Joint Governor
Henry Hawley	1666 Joint Governor
Samuel Barwick	1666 Joint Governor
William, Lord Willoughby	1667
Sir Jonathan Atkins	1674
Sir Richard Dutton	1680
James Kendal	1690
Francis Russell	1695
Hon. Ralph Grey	1698
Sir Bevil Granville	1703
Mitford Crowe	1707
Robert Lowther	1711
Henry Worsley	1722
Scroop, Viscount Howe	1733
Hon. Robert Byng	1739
Sir Thomas Robinson, Bart.	1742
Hon. Henry Grenville	1747
Charles Pinfold	1756
William Spry	1768
Hon. Edward Hay	1773
James Cunningham	1780
David Parry	1784
George Poyntz Ricketts	1794
Francis Humberstone Mackenzie, Lord Seaforth	1801
Sir George Beckwith, K.B.	1810
Sir James Leith, K.B.	1815
Stapleton, Viscount Combermere, G.C.B.	1817
Sir Henry Warde, K.C.B.	1821
Sir James Lyon, K.C.B.	1829

Sir Lionel Smith, K.C.B.	1833
Sir Evan McGregor, Bart., K.C.B.	1836
Sir Charles Edward Grey	1841
Sir William Reid, K.C.B.	1846
Sir William Colebrooke	1848
Sir Francis Hincks, K.C.M.G., C.B.	1856
Sir James Walker, K.C.M.G., C.B.	1862
Sir Rawson W. Rawson, K.C.M.G., C.B.	1866
Sir John Pope Henessey, K.C.M.G.	1875
Sir George Strahan, K.C.M.G.	1876
Sir William Robinson, K.C.M.G.	1880
Sir C.C. Lees, K.C.M.G.	1885
Sir Walter Sendall, K.C.M.G.	1889
Sir James Hay, K.C.M.G.	1892
Sir Frederick Hodgson, K.C.M.G.	1900
Sir Gilbert Carter, K.C.M.G.	1904
Sir Leslie Probyn, K.C.M.G.	1911
Sir Charles O'Brien, K.C.M.G.	1918
Sir William Robertson, K.C.M.G.	1925
Harry Scott Newlands, C.M.G.	1933
Sir Mark Aitchinson Young, K.C.M.G.	1933
Sir John Waddington, K.C.M.G.	1938
Sir Henry Grattan Bushe, K.C.M.G.	1941
Sir Hilary Blood, K.C.M.G.	1947
Sir Alfred Savage, K.C.M.G.	1949
Sir Robert Arundell, K.C.M.G.	1953
Sir John Montague Stow, K.C.M.G.	1959–1966

Appendix 6

Names on the eleven surviving *Bonds for Tickets to Depart the Island* 21 March 1766 to 12 April 1766, held at the BDA under Ref: RB9/2/2

Name and parish of traveler	Names and parishes of those giving surety
George Trehern, St Michael	Hacket Malloney, Giles Reece, both of St Michael
Jacobes Vangilsh, St Michael	Benjamin Nicolls, Samuel Went, both of St Michael
Benjamin Sullivan, St Michael	Saml. Lightfoot, William Willoughby, both of St Michael
Archibald Armour, St John	Thomas Armour, St John, Morris Morrison, St Michael
Charles Gray, St Michael	Val Jones, John Scott, both of St Michael
Cholmley Callin, St Michael	Samuel Went, Richard King, both of St Michael
Richard Sims, St Michael	Thos Applewhaite, Darby Lux, both of St Michael
Simeon Kellman, St Peter	John Clark Ford, St Michael, Matthew Boyce, Island of St Lucia
Roger Smith, St Michael	John Haslen, Henry Fisher, both of St Michael
John Boone, St Michael	Samuel Kerr, Thomas Tipping, both of St Michael
John Kinslow, St Michael	Samuel Kerr, Tho. Tipping, both of St Michael

Bibliography

Addinton Forde, G. *Place-Names of Barbados.* Barbados: Folklore Publications, 2003 (BML, NLS).

Aldersley, Cyril F. *The Moravians: Two Centuries of Work in Barbados.* Pamphlet (BDA).

Alleyne, Warren. *Barbados at War 1939–1945: A Historical Account.* Barbados: Coles Printery Ltd., 1999 (BDA, BML, NLS).

Alleyne, Warren. *Historic Bridgetown.* Barbados National Trust, 1978 (BDA, BML, NLS). New edition. Barbados Government Information Service, 2003 (BML).

Alleyne, Warren, and Henry Fraser. *The Barbados-Carolina Connection.* Oxford, England: Macmillan, 1988. Reprint. 2003 (BDA, BML, NLS).

Alleyne, Warren, and Jill Sheppard. *The Barbados Garrison and its Buildings.* Oxford, England: Macmillan Education Ltd., 1990 (BDA, BML, NLS).

Arbell, Mordechai. *The Jewish Nation of the Caribbean: The Spanish-Portuguese Jewish Settlements in the Caribbean and the Guianas.* Jerusalem, Israel: Gefen Publishing House, 2002.

Baldwin, Agnes Leland. *First Settlers of South Carolina 1670–1680.* Greenville, SC: Southern Historical Press, 1970 (BDA, BML).

Barbados Museum & Historical Society Journal. 1933 to date, published by the BMHS (BDA, BML, NLS).

Beckles, Hilary. *Black Rebellion in Barbados: The Struggle Against Slavery 1627–1838.* Caribbean Research Publications Inc., 1987 (BDA, BML, NLS).

Beckles, Hilary. *Bussa: The 1816 Barbados Revolution.* Dept. of History, the University of the West Indies & the Barbados Museum & Historical Society, 1998 (BDA, BML, NLS).

Beckles, Hilary. *A History of Barbados: from Amerindian settlement to nation-state.* Cambridge University Press, 1990 (BDA, BML, NLS).

Besse, Joseph. *Sufferings of Early Quakers: America–New England & Maryland, West Indies–Antigua Barbados Jamaica and Nevis, Bermuda.* 1753. Reprint. York, England: Ebor Press, 2001(BML).

Blackman, Francis W. (Woodie). *Methodism: 200 Years in Barbados.* Cedar Press, 1988 (BDA, BML, NLS).

Brandow, James C., compiler. *Genealogies of Barbados Families.* Baltimore, MD: Genealogical Publishing Co. Inc., 1982. Reprint. 2004 (BDA, BML).

Brandow, James C. *Omitted Chapters from Hotten's Original List of Persons of Quality.* Baltimore, MD: Genealogical Publishing Co. Inc., 1983. Reprint. 2004 (BDA, BML).

Campbell, P.F. *An Outline of Barbados History.* Barbados: Caribbean Graphics, 1974 (BDA, BML).

Campbell, P.F. *Some Early Barbadian History.* Caribbean Graphics & Letchworth Ltd., 1993 (BDA, BML, NLS).

Campbell, Tony. *The Printed Maps of Barbados.* Map Collectors' Circle, 1965 (BDA, BML, NLS).

Carrington, S., H. Fraser, J. Gilmore, and A. Forde. *A–Z of Barbados Heritage.* Heinemann (Caribbean) Ltd, 1990 (BDA, BML, NLS). New Edition. Oxford, England: Macmillan Caribbean, 2003 (BML).

Chandler, M.J. *A Guide to Records in Barbados.* Basil Blackwell for the University of the West Indies, 1965 (BDA, BML, NLS).

Coldham, Peter Wilson. *The Bristol Registers of Servants Sent to Foreign Plantations, 1654–1686.* Baltimore, MD: Genealogical Publishing Co. Inc., 1988.

Coldham, Peter Wilson. *The Complete Book of Emigrants 1607–1776.* 4 vols. Baltimore, MD: Genealogical Publishing Co. Inc., 1987–93.

Coldham, Peter Wilson. *The Complete Book of Emigrants in Bondage 1614–1775.* Baltimore, MD: Genealogical Publishing Co. Inc., 1988.

Coldham, Peter Wilson. *Supplement to The Complete Book of Emigrants in Bondage, 1614–1775.* Baltimore, MD: Genealogical Publishing Co. Inc., 1992.

Coldham, Peter Wilson. *English Convicts in Colonial America. Vol. 1, Middlesex 1617–1775.* New Orleans, LA: Polyanthos, 1974 (BDA, BML).

D'Arcy McGee, Thomas. *A History of the Irish Settlers in North America.* 1852. Reprint. Baltimore, MD: Genealogical Publishing Co. Inc., 2003.

Darnell Davis, N. *Cavaliers & Roundheads of Barbados 1650–1652.* Argosy Press, 1887 (BDA, BML).

Dobson, David. *Barbados and Scotland, Links 1627–1877.* Baltimore, MD: Clearfield Company Inc., 2005 (BML).

Dobson, David. *Directory of Scots Banished to the American Plantations 1650–1775.* 1983. Reprint. Baltimore, MD: Clearfield Company Inc., 2005 (BML).

Dobson, David. *The Original Scots Colonists of Early America: Caribbean supplement 1611–1707.* Baltimore, MD: Genealogical Publishing Co. Inc., 1999.

Dobson, David. *Scots in the West Indies 1707–1857.* Baltimore, MD: Clearfield Company Inc., 2002.

Dobson, David. *Scottish Emigration to Colonial America, 1607–1785.* University of Georgia Press, 2004.

Dunn, Richard S. *Sugar & Slaves: The Rise of the Planter Class in the English West Indies, 1624–1713.* University of North Carolina Press, 1972 (BDA, BML, NLS).

Durham, Harriet Frorer. *Caribbean Quakers.* Hollywood, FL: Dukane Press Inc., 1972 (BDA, BML).

Dyde, Brian. *The Empty Sleeve: The Story of the West India Regiments of the British Army.* London, England: Hansib Caribbean, 1997 (BDA, BML, NLS).

Fothergill, Gerald. *Emigrant Ministers to America 1690–1811.* Elliot Stock, 1904 (BML).

Fraser, H.S. and R. Hughes. *Historic Houses of Barbados.* Barbados National Trust, 1986 (BDA, BML, NLS).

Gandy, Wallace. *The Association Oath Rolls of the British Plantations 1696.* 1922. Reprint. Baltimore, MD: Clearfield Company Inc., 1996 (BDA).

Ghirelli, Michael. *A List of Emigrants from England to America 1682–1692.* Magna Carta Book Company, 1968. Reprint. Baltimore, MD: Clearfield Company Inc., 1989 (BDA, BML).

Gleadall, Mary E. *Monumental Inscriptions in the Barbados Military Cemetery.* gleadallm@caribsurf.com (BDA, BML).

Goddard, Richard B., compiler. *George Washington's Visit to Barbados 1751.* Barbados: Coles Printery Ltd., 1997 (BDA, BML).

Grannum, Guy. *Tracing Your West Indian Ancestors.* London, England: Public Record Office, 1995. 2nd ed. 2002 (BDA, BML 1995 Ed.).

Greenidge, Morris. *Holetown Barbados: Settlement Revisited.* Barbados: MG Events, 2003 (BDA, BML, NLS).

Handler, J.S. *Guide to Source Materials for the Study of Barbados History, 1627–1834.* South Illinois University Press, 1971. Reprint. New Castle, DE: Oak Knoll Press, 2002 (BDA, BML, NLS).

Handler, J.S. *Supplement to A Guide to Source Materials for the Study of Barbados History, 1627–1834.* Providence, RI: The John Carter Brown Library, 1991. Reprint. New Castle, DE: Oak Knoll Press, 2002 (BDA, BML, NLS).

Handler, J.S. *Plantation Slavery in Barbados: An Archaeological & Historical Investigation.* Cambridge, MA: Harvard University Press, 1978 (BDA, BML, NLS).

Handler, J.S. *The Unappropriated People: Freedmen in the Slave Society of Barbados.* Baltimore, MD: Johns Hopkins University Press, 1974 (BDA, BML, NLS).

Handler, Jerome S., and JoAnn Jacoby. *Slave Names and Naming in Barbados 1650–1830. The William & Mary Quarterly,* 3rd Series, vol. 53, no.4. Oct 1996 (BDA, BML).

Handler, J.S., R. Hughes, and E.M. Wiltshire. *Freedmen of Barbados: Names & Notes for Genealogical & Family History Research.* Friends of the Barbados Archives, 1999 (BDA, BML, NLS).

Hill, Barbara. *Historic Churches of Barbados.* Edited by H.S. Fraser. Barbados: Art Heritage Publications, 1984 (BDA, BML, NLS).

Hotten, J.C. *Original Lists of Persons of Quality...and Others Who Went from Great Britain to the American Plantations, 1600–1700.* 1874. Reprint. Baltimore, MD: Clearfield Company Inc., 2004 (BDA, BML).

Hoyos, F.A. *Barbados: A History from the Amerindians to Independence.* Oxford, England: Macmillan Press, 1992 (BDA, BML, NLS).

Kaminkow, Jack, and Marion Kaminkow. *Original Lists of Emigrants in Bondage from London to the American Colonies 1719–1744.* Baltimore, MD: Magna Carta Book Company, 1967 (BDA).

Kent, D.L. *Barbados & America.* Carol M. Kent, 1980. www.candoo.com/projects/banda.html (BDA, BML, NLS).

Lewis, K. *The Moravian Mission in Barbados 1816–1886: A Study of the Historical Context and Theological Significance of a Minority Church Among an Oppressed People.* New York: Verlag Peter Lang, 1985 (BDA, BML, NLS).

Lynch, James, compiler. *Old Barbados Newspapers.* 2000. www.candoo.com/projects/newspapers.htm (BML).

McDonnell, Frances. *Highland Jacobites 1745.* Baltimore, MD: Genealogical Publishing Co. Inc., 2002 (BML).

Newton, Velma. *The Silver Men: West Indian Labour Migration to Panama 1850–1914.* Sir Arthur Lewis Institute of Social & Economic Research, 1984. New edition. Jamaica: Ian Randle Publishers, 2004 (BDA, BML, NLS 1984 Ed.).

Nicholson, Cregoe D.P. *Some Early Emigrants to America and Early Emigrants to America from Liverpool.* Baltimore, MD: Clearfield Company Inc., 1989 (BDA).

O'Callaghan, Sean. *To Hell or Barbados: The Ethnic Cleansing of Ireland.* Dingle, Co. Kerry, Ireland: Mount Eagle Publications, 2000 (BML).

Oliver, Vere Langford. *Caribbeana.* 1910–1919, 6 vols. (BDA, BML, NLS). Reprint. James Lynch, 2000. www.candoo.com/olivers/caribbeana.html (BML).

Oliver, Vere Langford. *The Monumental Inscriptions in the Churches & Churchyards of the Island of Barbados,* 1915. Reprint. San Bernardino, CA: The Borgo Press, 1995 (BDA, BML, NLS).

Pomery, Chris. *DNA and Family History.* London, England: The National Archives, 2004.

Reece, Rev Canon J.E., and Rev Canon C.G. Clark-Hunt. *Barbadian Diocesan History.* The West India Committee, 1925 (BDA, BML, NLS).

Roberts, G.W. *Emigration from the Island of Barbados.* Journal of Social & Economic Studies, vol. 4, no.3, 1955 (BML).

Salazar, L.E. *Love Child: A Genealogist's Guide to the Social History of Barbados.* familyfind@caribsurf.com, 2000 (BDA, BML, NLS).

Sanders, Joanne McRee. *Barbados Records: Baptisms 1637–1800.* Sanders Historical Publications. Reprint. Baltimore, MD: Genealogical Publishing Co. Inc, 1984 (BDA, BML, NLS).

Sanders, Joanne McRee. *Barbados Records: Marriages 1643–1800.* 2 vols. Sanders Historical Publications. Reprint. Baltimore, MD: Genealogical Publishing Co. Inc., 1982 (BDA, BML, NLS).

Sanders, Joanne McRee. *Barbados Records: Wills & Administrations 1639–1725.* 3 vols. Sanders Historical Publications. Reprint. Baltimore, MD: Genealogical Publishing Co. Inc., 1979–1981 (BDA, BML, NLS).

Sheppard, Jill. *The "Redlegs" of Barbados: Their Origins and History.* New York: KTO Press, 1977 (BDA, BML, NLS).

Shilstone, Eustace M. *Monumental Inscriptions in the Burial Ground of the Jewish Synagogue at Bridgetown, Barbados.* New York: 1956 (BDA, BML, NLS).

Sykes, Bryan. *The Seven Daughters of Eve.* London, England: Bantam, 2001.

Titus, Noel F. *The Development of Methodism in Barbados 1823–1883.* New York: Peter Lang Inc., 1994 (BDA, NLS).

Wareing, John. *Emigrants to America: Indentured Servants Recruited in London 1718–1733.* 1985. Reprint. Baltimore, MD: Clearfield Company Inc., 2002 (BML).

Watson, Karl. *The Civilised Island Barbados: A Social History 1750–1816.* Barbados: 1979 (BDA, BML, NLS).

Watson, Karl. *A Kind of Right to be Idle: Old Doll Matriarch of Newton Plantation.* The Barbados Museum & Historical Society and the University of the West Indies, 2000 (BDA, BML, NLS).

Welch, Pedro L.V. *Slave Society in the City: Bridgetown Barbados 1680–1834.* Jamaica: Ian Randle Publishers, 2003 (BDA, BML, NLS).

Welch, Pedro L.V. *"What's in a Name?": From Slavery to Freedom in Barbados.* Paper presented to the Forum, Dept. of History, University of the West Indies, Cave Hill, Barbados, 2003 (BDA).

Welch, Pedro L.V. with Richard A. Goodridge. *"Red" & Black over White: Free Coloured Women in Pre- Emancipation Barbados.* Carib Research & Publications Inc., 2000 (BDA, BML, NLS).

INDEX